MW01077635

A

MANUAL OF PRAYERS

FOR THE

USE OF THE SCHOLARS

OF

WINCHESTER COLLEGE,

BY THE

RIGHT REV. THOMAS KEN, D. D.

LATE LORD BISHOP OF BATH AND WELLS

A NEW EDITION

OXFORD:

JOHN HENRY PARKER.

M.DCCC XL

MEMOIR

OF

BISHOP KEN.

THOMAS KEN, the admirable Author of this little book, was born at Berkhampstead in Hertfordshire, in July 1637. In his fifteenth year he was sent to Winchester College, where he was admitted, as appears by the register of the College, on the 30th of January 1651. It would seem, however, from various circumstances, that there is a clerical error in this entry, and that he was admitted in Jan. 1652. His name is still to be seen, cut in the stone, on a buttress in the south east corner of the college cloisters, THO. KEN, 1656. Among his schoolfellows was Francis Turner, afterwards Bishop of Ely, to whom he was most warmly attached. The friendship of these two excellent men lasted all their lives, who were in many remarkable re-

spects united together. They were both raised to
the episcopal dignity, and nearly at the same time.
They both attended the death-bed of King Charles
II. and the scaffold of his unfortunate son the
Duke of Monmouth. They were both of the
number of the seven Bishops whose famous re-
sistance of the dispensing power claimed by James
II. was one of the main and immediate causes of
the Revolution; and they both submitted to "the
loss of all which they could not keep with a good
conscience," being deprived of the honours and
emoluments of their Bishoprics because they refused
to take the new oaths of allegiance. In the later
correspondence of Bishop Ken there are several
affectionate references to the memory of his old
schoolfellow and "deare friend the Bishop of Ely,
now with God." It is a pleasing reflection, that
the friendship of these admirable men, thus begun
when boys, when doubtless "they took sweet
counsel together, and walked in the house of God
as friends," lasted on through all the vicissitudes
of earthly fortune, till by the grace of God it
strengthened them for their great duty of confessors
of God's truth, and champions of His Church,
to which they were called together.

Of Ken's life and behaviour during his boyish

years we have no account. But if we may suppose him to have endeavoured to serve God himself, as by this little book he desires to bring others to serve Him, (a supposition which the grace and goodness of his after-life make highly reasonable,) we may believe him to have given a lovely specimen of an early piety. An early piety! "than which" (he says, addressing a Winchester scholar, p. 4,) "nothing will make you a greater comfort to all your friends, or a greater blessing to the very College where you are bred: nothing will make you more universally esteemed and beloved by all men, or more successful in your studies." We have good reason to think, from his subsequent character, that such an early piety was exhibited in himself, and that the comfort and blessing here spoken of, did indeed, by God's mercy, abound to all those who were happy enough to be so connected with him.

From Winchester College Ken was removed to Hart Hall in Oxford, and from thence, after a few months, he became scholar, and then fellow, of New College. After nine years spent at Oxford, during which he took the degree of Master of Arts, and entered into Holy Orders, he returned to the place of his early education, being chosen a Fellow of Winchester College on the 8th of Dec. 1666.

Once more restored to his beloved Winchester, he seems to have spent some years in great peace and profit. He was soon taken notice of by Dr. George Morley, then Bishop of Winchester, who presented him to the living of Woodhay, near Newbury, and made him his domestic Chaplain. The Bishop had then newly rebuilt the palace of Wolvesey, which is very near the College of Winchester, and which in the times of the vacancy of the see, had fallen very much into decay. In this hospitable home dwelt the excellent Isaac Walton, the now widowed husband of Ken's sister, who, having entertained Morley in his quiet cottage near Stafford during the dismal period of the usurpation, was now willing to share his friend's prosperity on the return of happier days. This relationship, and the office held by Ken in the Bishop's family, gave him constant and familiar access to this cheerful circle; and we may easily conceive how peaceably and profitably his days would be spent, while he enjoyed the opportunity of varying the tranquillity and studious habits of his college life, with the cheerful and improving society of the Bishop's family. It was at this time that he composed his Manual of Prayers for the use of Winchester scholars.

He was an exact economist of his time; and it is related of him by his biographer and great nephew Hawkins, that he strictly accustomed himself to one sleep only in the night, so that he often rose at one or two o'clock in the morning. It was also his regular practice to sing his morning hymn to the lute before he put on his clothes. It is very interesting to find that it was from his own experience of the happy effects of this habit that he recommended it to the scholars of Winchester College, (vide p. 6,) and composed the three well known hymns, printed at the end of this little volume, for their use.

In the year 1669 he was made Prebendary of Winchester, and after some years Chaplain in ordinary to King Charles II., and Chaplain to Mary Princess of Orange. In both these situations he was called upon to shew his firm and honest zeal for truth and virtue, and to exhibit in his own person the qualities of which he speaks in his admirable sermon on the character of Daniel; "faithfulness in the discharge of his duty both to king and people, remoteness from all flattery, courage on just and fit occasions, in warning his great

masters of their dangers, and minding them of
their duty." He incurred the serious displeasure
of the Prince of Orange by promoting the marriage
of a young lady of the court with Count Zulestein
the Prince's uncle, and was only induced to remain
in his office by the earnest entreaty of the Prince
and Princess themselves. And on one occasion,
when King Charles II. came to Winchester, and
his harbinger had marked Dr. Ken's house for the
use of the notorious Mrs. Eleanor Gwyn, he absolutely refused her admission, alleging that a woman
of ill repute ought not to be endured in the house
of a clergyman, especially of the King's Chaplain.
His refusal was so peremptory, that it was found
necessary to erect a small building at the south
end of the Deanery, then occupied by the King,
for her temporary accommodation, which building
was long known by the name of Nell Gwyn, and
has only been removed within the present century.
This honest boldness was so far from offending the
King, that on the vacancy of the See of Bath and
Wells, which fell very shortly after, it is said that
the King put aside all applications which were
made to him in behalf of several other persons,
and expressed his determination to give it to Ken
in these words, "Odd's Fish! who shall have

Bath and Wells but the little fellow who would not give poor Nelly a lodging?"

Dr. Ken was accordingly consecrated Bishop of Bath and Wells, by Archbishop Sancroft, on St. Paul's day, 1684. No sooner, however, was he thus raised, by the Providence of God turning the caprice of a wicked King to His own holy purposes, than he was called upon to discharge the most solemn office of ministerial faithfulness to the Sovereign by whose favour he was so recently promoted. He, together with the Archbishop of Canterbury, and the Bishops of London, Durham, and Ely, attended the death-bed of Charles, who was struck with fatal sickness in the beginning of February, and died within a week of his seizure. It is recorded by Hawkins, that Bishop Ken remained in attendance by the King's bedside for three days and nights without intermission; and that he prevailed upon the King to have the Duchess of Portsmouth removed from the royal chamber, and to ask the forgiveness of his injured Queen. Bishop Burnet too, who was both the political and personal enemy of Bishop Ken, writes, that "he applied himself to the awakening of the King's conscience, and spoke with a great elevation both of thought and expression, like a man in-

spired, as those who were present told me." He
endeavoured in vain to prevail on the King to take
the Holy Sacrament. At length he was desired to
retire, and the King, who had for some time been
secretly devoted to the Popish faith, received extreme unction from the hands of Huddleston a
Romish priest.

On the accession of James II. Bishop Ken went
down to Wells to undertake his episcopal duties.
Of his behaviour in his diocese we have the best
testimony in the affectionate respect with which his
memory has ever since been held in the Church.
He lost no opportunity of instructing the people.
He preached often, and published several small
pieces, such as his Exposition of the Church
Catechism, with directions for Prayer, and a Pastoral Letter to his Clergy concerning their behaviour in Lent. In these publications, as in all his
other remains, he shews his primitive and simple
faith. At a time when licentiousness was estrang-
ing a large portion of the laity from Christian faith
and practice, and a dangerous spirit of latitudina-
rianism was growing up among many of the Clergy,
Bishop Ken was one of the most strenuous and in-
fluential supporters of Church doctrines and usages.
His life, from his youth, had been one of constant

self-denial and mortification. His fastings and watchings, his primitive prayers and communions, could not be entirely unknown; and while they attracted the respectful affection of those who, though they did not practise them themselves, still could recognise their fitness and value in another, they prepared him for the great exercises of self denial in his life, to which he was called. Thus his Christian self-government and discipline were the secret of his strength, as his free and almost unlimited almsgiving was the preparation of his cheerful contentment in his own reverses.

Shortly after he took up his residence at Wells, the unhappy battle of Sedgemoor took place, in which the rebellion of the misguided Duke of Monmouth was entirely crushed. The field of battle was within a day's journey of Wells, where the Bishop, whose interposition had already checked the murderous revenge of the conquerors, received the unhappy fugitives by hundreds, and extended to them his free and Christian charity. When the Duke was soon after taken prisoner, and sentenced to death, Ken was appointed, together with Bishop Turner of Ely, and Doctors Hooper and Tenison, to attend him on the scaffold. But their holy counsel was once more in great measure ineffectual.

They endeavoured in vain to prevail on the Duke
to acknowledge the guilt of his rebellion. He died
with a general expression of forgiveness and repentance, but without making more particular refer-
ence to his recent attempt.   For their endeavours
to persuade the Duke to a more express confession
of his guilt in this respect, the two Bishops have
been most severely and unjustly blamed.

When the famous Declaration of Liberty of Conscience was ordered by King James II. to be read
in all the Churches, Bishop Ken, with Archbishop
Sancroft, Bishops Lake of Chichester, Turner of
Ely, Lloyd of St. Asaph, Trelawney of Bristol,
and White of Peterborough, joined in addressing
a humble petition to His Majesty, representing the
illegality of the dispensing power therein claimed,
and their unwillingness to sanction it by such a
publication. For this offence they were tried at
Westminster for a seditious libel.   But the attempts
of James to restore Popery had now so thoroughly
alarmed the whole country, that the utmost feeling
of indignation against the court, and sympathy
for the Bishops was excited by this outrageous
prosecution. As the Bishops were conveyed to
the Tower in boats from Westminster, "the whole
shore," says Hume, "was covered with crowds of

prostrate spectators, who at once implored the blessing of these holy pastors, and addressed their petitions towards Heaven for protection during this extreme danger, to which their country and their religion
stood exposed. Even the soldiers, seized with the
contagion of the same spirit, flung themselves on
their knees before the distressed prelates, and craved
the benediction of those criminals whom they were
appointed to guard. Some persons ran into the
water that they might participate more nearly of
those blessings which the prelates were distributing
on all around them." The verdict of acquittal
was received with loud shouts of joy. It happened
that the King had just been reviewing the troops
at Hounslow, and had retired into Lord Feversham's
tent, when he was surprised to hear a great uproar
in the camp, attended with the most extravagant
symptoms of tumultuary joy. He suddenly in-
quired the cause, and was told by Feversham, " It
was nothing but the rejoicing of the soldiers for
the acquittal of the Bishops." " Do you call that
nothing ?" replied he, "but so much the worse
for them."

When James had fled and the Prince of Orange
had landed, Bishop Ken, with all the other Prelates, except two, was very earnest in his place

in parliament that a Regent should be appointed
with royal authority, the succession remaining
unchanged; or that if the throne should be de-
clared vacant, the Princess Mary, as the next
heir, should be called to fill it. When, however,
these proposals were thrown out, he retired to his
diocese, there to await the settlement of affairs in
which he could no longer conscientiously take
part.

On the passing of the bill for settling the crown
on the Prince and Princess of Orange conjointly,
the sole administration being reserved to the
Prince, Bishop Ken, with many other Clergy and
Laymen, felt that he had no warrant in conscience
for transferring his allegiance to a new monarch
who could assign no title to the throne but a mere
election. He therefore declined to take the new
oaths which were imposed, and preferred to lose
all and retire to poverty rather than violate his
conscience. Five of the seven Bishops who had
resisted the dispensing power of James were found
among the non-jurors, thus exhibiting the noble
spectacle of men who could at once maintain their
duty in defiance of the utmost anger and persecu-
tion of their Sovereign, and yet lose all their
worldly means and prospects rather than disown

their real and true allegiance. Unhappily there were found those who were willing to succeed to the deprived Bishops, and thus to acknowledge the power of the State to break off the episcopal succession, and sever the connection between a Bishop and his Diocese. Bishop Ken made a public protest against his deprivation, asserting from his pastoral chair in the Cathedral of Wells, his canonical right, and professing that he esteemed himself still the canonical Bishop of the Diocese, and that he would be ready on all occasions to perform his pastoral duties. The See was then offered to Dr. Beveridge, by whom it was declined, and Dr. Kidder was appointed to it.

Thus reduced to poverty, for his income on his deprivation was twenty pounds a year, Bishop Ken found an asylum in the house of his nephew, Isaac Walton, Canon of Salisbury, and Rector of Polshot near Devizes. In this family he passed the greater part of his remaining years, keeping up a kind fraternal intercourse with his deprived brethren, and doing all in his power to minister to their wants. On one occasion, a charitable design of this kind, set on foot by the pious Mr. Kettlewell, caused him to be summoned before the Privy Council and examined; but not the slightest suspicion ever rested on him of being involved in any plots against the peace of the country, or in favour of the exiled family, though we know that he was much solicited to join in them.

In the year 1708 a violent storm visited the whole of the West of England. Bishop Ken very narrowly escaped with his life, but a stack of chimneys blown down in the Palace of Wells crushed to death the intruding Bishop Kidder and his wife in the ruins. This event appeared to offer an opportunity of healing in part the unhappy schism which tore in pieces the Church in England, and had separated many of the most pious and excellent of the Clergy from the National Communion. Bishop Ken, therefore, hearing that Dr. Hooper, Bishop of St. Asaph, who had formerly been his fellow chaplain to Bishop Morley, and in whose character and principles he had full confidence, was likely to be appointed to succeed Dr. Kidder, but was unwilling to accept the appointment out of delicacy to him, wrote him an urgent letter, pressing him to allow himself to be translated to Bath and Wells, and promising to make a cession of his canonical rights in his favour. This cession, which he accordingly made, was highly displeasing to many of the other deprived clergy, and Bishop

Ken was blamed with no little severity for his conduct in it. Whatever judgment, however, may be passed upon the act itself, there can be no doubt that Ken was actuated by the purest feelings of charity and love of peace in performing it.

This was the last event of public consequence in the life of this great and good man. He died at Longleat on the 19th of March, 1710, at the age of seventy-three, and was buried in the churchyard of Frome in Somersetshire, leaving behind him the name of one of the most primitive and holy Bishops, who, by God's mercy, have been raised up to adorn the Apostolical Church in England.

In page 7, and in one or two other passages of this little book, the phrase occurs of " going Circum." This expression is now quite obsolete and forgotten. It appears, however, that in the schooldays of the oldest living Wykehamists, the small passage leading to the chapel and cloisters of the College was open to the boys, with a bench round it placed close to the walls. It was the practice of the boys, on coming out of school at six o'clock, to go into this passage, and, stooping or kneeling down by the bench, to say their short private prayers; and this practice was still called "going Circum." Possibly, in former times, the boys may have walked in procession round the cloisters after schooltime, singing one of the old church hymns, still extant among them, and when this usage came to be considered Popish, they may have been confined to the dark entrance passage, and their separate voluntary prayers. From the dates of the names cut on the walls of the cloisters, it seems as if they were first opened for the ordinary secular use of the boys about the time of the puritanical Warden Harris, when Bishop Ken first came to school; and shut up altogether from them soon after the beginning of the next century.

G. M.

Winchester College,
Dec. 11, 1839.

A

MANUAL OF PRAYERS

FOR THE

USE OF THE SCHOLARS OF WINCHESTER COLLEGE.

———

AN EXHORTATION TO YOUNG PHILOTHEUS.

IF you have any regard, good Philotheus, to your own eternal happiness, it ought to be your chiefest care to serve and glorify God. It is for this end God both made and redeemed you; and two excellent rules He hath given you in Holy Scripture, by the conscientious observation of which you will be able, through His grace, to dedicate your tender years to His glory.

The one teaches you what you are to do,
" Remember now thy Creator in the days of
" thy youth." [a]

The other teaches you what you are to avoid,
" Flee youthful lusts ;" that is, all those sins
which are usually incident to young persons. [b]

You cannot imagine the unspeakable advan-
tages a pious youth gains by the practice of
these two rules ; and how many ghostly
dangers that soul escapes, which is seasoned
betimes with the fear of God, before he is
sullied with ill company, before he hath contracted vicious habits, which will cost him
infinite pains to unlearn, before his affections
are too far engaged in the world, to be easily
recalled, and before the devil hath got too
strong a hold in him, to be suddenly dispos-
sessed.

O Philotheus, do but ask any one old
penitent, what fruit, what satisfaction he hath
purchased to himself, by all those pleasures of
sin which flattered him in his youth, and of
which he is now ashamed. Will he not sadly

tell you, he has found them all to be but vanity
and vexation of spirit? How will he befool
himself, for the many good opportunities he
hath lost, and wish a thousand times that he
were to live over his misspent days again!
And how bitterly will he, with David, bewail
the sins of his youth. [c]

Learn then, good Philotheus, by the dear-
bought experience of others, to accustom yourself to bear Christ's yoke from your youth,
and His yoke will sit easy on your neck; for
your duty will grow natural to you by beginning betimes.

Do but consider, how welcome a young
convert is to God; it was to young Samuel
that God revealed Himself, and that at such a
time too, when the word of God was preciou
and very rare, to shew how much God
honoured a young prophet, [d] and you know
that St. John, the youngest of all the disciples,
is the only person of all the twelve, who was
permitted to lean on our Saviour's bosom, at
the last supper, as dearest to Him in affection,

c Ps. xxv. 6.   d 1 Sam. iii. 1.

and who is emphatically called the disciple whom Jesus loved : ^e and this is suitable to that gracious promise which God hath made to encourage all young persons to serve Him : " I love them that love Me, and they that seek Me early shall find Me^f.

O Philotheus, let this heavenly promise excite in you a great zeal to seek God, and seek Him early : for if you do seek, you are sure to find Him; you are sure, when you have found Him, He will love you; and you shall reap all the happy effects of God's infinite love, and of an early piety.

An early piety! than which, nothing will make you a greater comfort to all your friends, or a greater blessing to the very college where you are bred; nothing will make you more universally esteemed, and beloved by all men, or more successful in your studies : and besides that peace of conscience, and the pleasure of well-doing you will at present feel; think, if you can, how unconceivable a joy it will be to you when, in your

e John xiii 23.   f Prov. viii. 17.

elder years, you can reflect on your well-spent time, and the innocence of your youth; how great a consolation it will be to you on your death-bed, how easy it will render your accompts at the great day of judgment, and how much a whole life spent in God's service, will increase your glory in heaven.

God of His great mercy, Philotheus, make these and the like considerations effectual to create holy resolutions in you, and give you grace to make good use of these following directions, which are designed to teach you to fear the Lord from your youth, and are suited to your particular age and condition, in hopes they may the more affect you. God grant they may.ᵍ Amen.

DIRECTIONS IN GENERAL,

As soon as ever you awake in the morning, good Philotheus, strive as much as you can, to keep all worldly thoughts out of

g 1 Kings xviii. 13.

your mind, till you have presented the first fruits of the day to God, which will be an excellent preparative to make you spend the rest of it the better; and therefore be sure to sing the morning and evening hymn in your chamber devoutly, remembering that the psalmist, upon happy experience assures you, that it is a good thing to tell of the lovingkindness of the Lord early in the morning, and of His truth in the night season. [h]

When you are ready, look on your soul as still undressed, till you have said your prayers.

Remember that God under the law or-dained a lamb to be offered up to Him every morning and evening. A lamb! which is a fit emblem of youth and innocence: think then that you are to resemble this lamb, and be sure every day to offer up yourself a morning and evening sacrifice to God. [i]

If you are a commoner, you may say your prayers in your own chamber; but if

h Ps. xcii. 1.   i Exod. xxix. 38.

you are a child, or a chorister, then, to avoid
the interruptions of the common chambers,
go into the chapel, between first and second
peal, in the morning, to say your morning
prayers, and to say your evening prayers when
you go Circum.

Now that every one may have this duty
proportioned to his capacity, the best way
is to distinguish two degrees of young Christians in this college, namely, those that
are of an age capable of receiving the holy
sacrament, and those that are not; and in
one of these two degrees you are to rank
yourself.

DIRECTIONS FOR THE YOUNGEST.

If you are very young, good Philotheus,
that God's commands may not seem grievous
to you at your first setting out, I shall advise
you to no more than your infant devotion
will bear; and that is, to take great care
to learn your catechism without book, and
to learn to understand it; for it is impossible

you can ever perform your duty, unless you
first know what it is; it is impossible you can
ever go to heaven, unless you learn the way
thither: and that you may beg God's daily
blessing, and His grace to assist you, learn
these two short prayers by heart, and say
them every day.

MORNING PRAYER.

Glory be to Thee, O Lord God, for all
the blessings I daily receive from Thee, and
for Thy particular preservation, and refresh-
ment of me, this night past.

O Lord, have mercy upon me, and forgive whatsoever Thou hast seen amiss in
me this night; and for the time to come
give me grace to fly all youthful lusts, and
to remember Thee, my Creator, in the days
of my youth.

Shower down Thy graces and blessings
on me, and on my relations, [on my father
and mother, on my brethren and sisters,]
on all my friends, on all my governors in

this place, and on all my fellow scholars, and give Thy angels charge over us, to protect us all from sin and danger.

Lord, bless me in my learning this day, that I may every day grow more fit for Thy service: O pardon my failings, and do more for me than I can ask, or think, for the merits of Jesus my Saviour, in Whose holy words I sum up all my wants. Our Father, Which art in heaven, &c.

EVENING PRAYER.

Glory be to Thee, O Lord God, for all the blessings I daily receive from Thee, and for Thy particular preservation of me this day.

O Lord, have mercy upon me, and forgive whatsoever Thou hast seen amiss in me this day past; and for the time to come give me grace to fly all youthful lusts, and to remember Thee my Creator in the days of my youth.

Lord, receive me and all my relations

and all that belong to this college, into Thy gracious protection this night, and send me such seasonable rest, that I may rise the next morning, more fit for Thy service.

Lord, hear my prayers, and pardon my failings, for the merits of my blessed Saviour, in Whose holy words I sum up all my wants.   Our Father, Which art in heaven, &c.

This, good Philotheus, is the lowest degree of duty, and it should be your daily endeavour to improve in your devotion, as well as in your learning, and the more effectually to move you to so happy an improvement, I advise you on Sundays and holydays attentively to read over the following meditation, and to propose to yourself, the Holy Child Jesus, for your example.

A MEDITATION ON THE HOLY CHILD JESUS.

Glory be to Thee, O Lord Jesus, glory be to Thee, Who when Thou wert twelve years old, didst go up to Jerusalem with Thy parents, after the custom of the feast, to eat the passover, and to worship Thy heavenly Father.[k]

O blessed Saviour, give me grace, like Thee, to make religion my first and chiefest care, and devoutly to observe all solemn times, and all holy rites, which relate to Thy worship.

Glory be to Thee, O Lord Jesus, glory be to Thee, Who when Thy parents returned home, didst stay behind in Jerusalem, and after three days, wast found of them in the temple, sitting in the midst of the doctors, both hearing them, and asking them questions.

O blessed Saviour, Who in Thy very childhood didst triumph over all the vain delights of youth, and wouldst choose no place but the temple to reside in, mortify in me all inordinate love of sensual pleasure, which may pervert me from my duty; raise in me an awful reverence of Thy house, an early devotion in my prayers, and a delight in Thy praises.

O blessed Jesu, Who didst choose, before

k Luke ii. 41.

all others, the company of the doctors, and
didst both hear them, and ask them questions;
give me grace to abhor all lewd company,
and all filthy communication; give me grace
to love wise, and sober, and profitable, and
religious conversation, and to be diligent
and inquisitive after learning, and whatsoever
is good.

Glory be to Thee, O Lord Jesus, glory be
to Thee, Who when Thy father and mother
had sought Thee sorrowing, didst reply to
them, "How is it that ye sought Me? Wist
ye not that I must be about My Father's
business?"

O blessed Jesu, Who from Thine infancy
didst make it Thy whole employment, to do
Thy Father's will, kindle in me a forward
zeal for Thy glory, that I may consecrate
my youth to Thy service, and make it the
great business of my life, to know and fear,
to love and obey my heavenly Father.

Glory be to Thee, O Lord Jesus, glory
be to Thee, Who didst at last return home
with Thy parents, and were subject to them.

O blessed Jesu, give me grace to honour my parents and governors, and readily to obey all their lawful commands !

Glory be to Thee, O Lord Jesus, glory be to Thee, Who in those tender years wert blessed with such heavenly wisdom, that all that heard Thee were astonished at Thy understanding and answers, Who didst daily increase in this heavenly wisdom, and in favour with God and man !

O Lord Jesu, bless me with all abilities of mind and body, that may make me daily increase in my learning ; but above all, bless me with wisdom from above, and give me Thy Holy Spirit to assist and enlighten me, that as I grow in age, I may daily grow in grace, and in the knowledge of Thee, and in favour with God and man, and every day more and more conformable to Thy unsinning and divine example. Amen, Lord Jesus, Amen.

DIRECTIONS FOR THOSE THAT ARE MORE GROWN IN YEARS.

When you have attained to more knowledge and proficiency in grace, and are of an age capable of receiving the Holy Sacrament, God then expects more from you; and it is high time for you, good Philotheus, to lengthen your prayers, and to begin to add some ejaculations over and above, such as these are, which follow.

EJACULATIONS AT WAKING OR RISING.

Awake, O my soul, and sing praises to God.

Glory be to Thee, O God, for watching over me this night.

Lord, raise me up at the last day, to life everlasting.

MORNING PRAYER

Early in the morning will I cry unto Thee; Lord, hear my prayer.

Glory be to Thee, Lord God Almighty; glory be to Thee, for renewing Thy mercies to me every morning; glory be to Thee, for refreshing me this night with sleep, and for preserving me from the perils of darkness.

O do away, as the night, so my transgressions; scatter my sins as the morning cloud!

Lord, forgive whatever Thou hast seen amiss in me this night, [my—*Here if you are conscious to yourself of any sin committed in the night, confess it.*] O Father of mercies, wash me throughly from my wickedness, and cleanse me from my sin.

And let Thy Holy Spirit so prevent, and accompany, and follow me this day, that I may believe in Thee, and love Thee, and keep Thy commandments, and continue in Thy fear all the day long.

Lord, make me chaste and temperate, humble and advisable, diligent in my studies, obedient to my superiors, and charitable to all men,

Lord, deliver me from sloth and idleness, from youthful lusts and ill company, from all dangers bodily and ghostly, and give me grace to remember Thee, my Creator, in the days of my youth.

Bless, and defend, and save the king, and all the royal family, and all orders of men amongst us, ecclesiastical or civil; Lord, give them all grace, in their several stations, to be instrumental to Thy glory, and the public good.

Together with them, I commend to Thy Divine Providence [*My father and mother, my brethren and sisters*] all my friends and relations, all my superiors in this place, and all my fellow scholars: O Lord, vouchsafe us all those graces and blessings which Thou knowest to be most suitable for us.

Unto Thee, O my God, do I dedicate this day, and my whole life; O do Thou so bless and prosper me in my studies, that I may every day grow more fit for Thy service.

Hear me, O Lord, and pardon my failings, for the merits of Thy Son Jesus, in Whose

holy words I sum up all my wants. Our
Father which art in heaven, &c.

DIRECTIONS FOR READING HOLY SCRIPTURE.

When you have said your morning prayer,
good Philotheus, you may then go cheerfully
to your study, and rely upon the Divine
goodness for a blessing.

But first, if you have time, I advise you
to read before second peal, some short Psalm,
or piece of a chapter out of the Gospel. or
historical books, because they are the most
easy to be understood; remembering the
example of young Timothy, who was bred
up to know the Scripture from a child.[1]

But if you want time on ordinary days
to read the Scripture, be sure to read
somewhat of it on Sundays and holidays,
and consider, that you have it daily read
to you in the hall before dinner and supper,
and at night when you are just going
to bed, that you may close the day with

1 2 Tim. iii. 15.

holy thoughts; and if you hearken diligently to it when it is read, you do in effect read it yourself.

Now to make your reading the more profitable to you, begin with one or more of these ejaculations.

EJACULATIONS BEFORE READING HOLY SCRIPTURE.

Wherewithal, Lord, shall a young man cleanse his way? even by ruling himself after Thy words.[m]

Lord, open my eyes, that I may see the wonderful things of Thy law.

O heavenly Father! I humbly beg Thy Holy Spirit so to help me at this time to read, and understand, and to remember, and practise Thy word, that it may make me wise to salvation.

When you are thus prepared, good Philotheus, then begin to read, and consider, that it is God's most holy word you read;

m Psalm cxix. 9. 18.

and that all the while you are reading, God is speaking to you, and therefore read with attention and humility, and endeavour as much as you can to suit your affections to the subject you read.

For instance, if you read any of God's commands, they should excite in you a zeal to keep them.

If you read any of God's threatenings against sinners, or His judgments on them, they should excite in you a fear to provoke Him.

When you read any of His gracious promises, they should encourage and quicken your obedience.

When you read any of God's mercies, they should excite you to thanksgiving.

When you read any great mystery recorded in holy writ, you are to prostrate your reason to divine revelation.

And to this purpose, in the midst of your reading, say,

Lord, give me grace to obey this command, or,

Lord, deliver me from this sin : or, this
   judgment : or,

Lord, I rely on this good promise : or,

Glory be to Thee, O Lord, for this mercy : or,

Lord, I believe and adore this mystery.

Say any of these, according as best agrees
with the subject you read ; and when you have
read as much as conveniently you can, conclude with one of these ejaculations.

EJACULATIONS AFTER READING.

" Blessed be Thou, O Lord, O teach me
Thy statutes! [n]

" Lord, make Thy word a lantern unto my
feet, and a light unto my paths.

" Lord, make Thy word my delight and my
counsellor."

DIRECTIONS FOR THE DAY-TIME.

O Philotheus, you cannot enough thank
God for the order of the place you live in,

n Psalm cxix.

where there is so much care taken to make you a good Christian, as well as a good scholar, where you go so frequently to prayers, every day in the chapel, and in the school; and sing hymns and psalms to God so frequently in your chamber, and in the chapel, and in the hall, so that you are in a manner brought up in a perpetuity of prayer.

Be sure, Philotheus, that you are accountable to God for all these opportunities He gives you of serving Him; and think how many blessings for yourself, and for the college you might obtain, if you prayed to and praised God rather out of a devout affection, than merely to comply with the custom of the place.

Prayer, good Philotheus, is the very life of a Christian, and therefore we are so frequently commanded to pray without ceasing: not that we can be always on our knees, but that we would accustom ourselves to frequent thoughts of God, that wheresoever we are, He sees us; and when we think on God, we should have always an ejaculation ready to offer up to Him, and by this means we may pray, not only seven times a day with David, but all the day long.°

In your reading Holy Scripture, especially in the Psalms, you may easily gather those short sentences which most affect you, for they are most proper for this use ; and when you have learned them without book, say one of them now and then, as they occur to your mind, or occasion requires, or as your devotion prompts you.

But be not troubled, if being otherwise lawfully employed, or if being indisposed, you pass a whole day without saying any, for to omit them is no sin ; nor be you scrupulous in what posture you say them ; for they being short breathings of the soul to God, requires not that solemnity, as set prayers do.

Now to give you some instances of ejaculatory prayer, take these following :

o Psalm cxix.

At going out.

" Lord, bless my going out, and my coming in, from this time forth for evermore." p

After a sin committed.

" Lord, be merciful to me, miserable sinner, and for the merits of my Saviour, lay not this sin to my charge."

After any Blessing or Deliverance.

" Glory be to Thee, O Lord, for this blessing, or, for this deliverance !

" Praise the Lord, O my soul, and all that is within me, praise His holy name." q

At giving Alms.

" O Lord, Who didst not despise the widow's mite, accept of this little I now give, to relieve one of Thy poor members." r

After having done any good.

" Not unto me, O Lord, not unto me, but unto Thy name be the praise." s

p Psalm cxxi. 8.   q Psalm ciii. 1.   r Mark xii. 42.
s Psalm cxv. 1.

In Temptation.

" Lord, succour me with Thy grace, that I may overcome this temptation."

DIRECTIONS FOR THE EVENING.

Consider, good Philotheus, how many that have gone to bed well over night have been found dead the next morning : and therefore it highly concerns you to take care to make your peace with God before you go to sleep.

I advise you therefore towards night, or when you go circum, to call yourself to an account how you have spent the day.

Examine your thoughts and discourses and actions, and recreations and devotions, and see what has been amiss in any of them.

Consider what idleness or unchastity, what lying and stubbornness you have been guilty of; or whether you have had a quarrel with any of your fellows ; and if you have, be sure to be friends with him before you say your prayers.

Again, consider what particular blessing, or deliverance God has vouchsafed you the day past, that you may give thanks for it, and then says as follows.

EVENING PRAYER.

"Let my prayer, O Lord, be set forth in Thy sight as incense, and the lifting up of my hands be as an evening sacrifice." t

Holy, holy, holy, Lord God, I miserable sinner humbly acknowledge that I have offended Thee this day, in thought, word, and deed, [particularly by—*here mention any sin you have been guilty of.*] But I fly into the arms of Thy Fatherly compassion; Lord, for Thy mercies' sake forgive me, cleanse me from my wickedness and strengthen my weakness, that I may overcome all the temptations which daily surround me, and continue constant in my obedience.

Accept of my humblest praise and thanks-

t Psalm cxli. 2.

giving, O Lord, for all the goodness Thou hast this day shewed me; for all the helps of preventing or restraining grace Thou hast vouchsafed me; for whatever I have done this day, which is in any measure acceptable to Thee, for whatever progress I have made in my study, for Thy preservation of me, from all the miseries and dangers which frail mortality is every moment exposed to, (particularly—*here name any particular blessing or deliverance God has sent you.*)

Praise the Lord, O my soul, Who saveth thy life from destruction, and crowneth thee with mercy and lovingkindness.

O heavenly Father, to Thy almighty protection I recommend myself and all my relations, and all that belong to this college; O Thou that never slumberest nor sleepest, watch over us, to preserve us from sin and danger.

Lord, let it be Thy good pleasure to refresh me this night with such seasonable rest, that I may rise the next morning more fit for Thy service; O pardon my failings, and hear my prayers, for the sake of my blessed Saviour, in

Whose holy words I sum up all my wants,
Our Father, &c.

EJACULATIONS AT GOING TO BED.

Lord, as I now go to my bed, I must one day go to my grave. O make me wise to consider my latter end.

I will lay me down in peace, and take my rest, for it is Thou, Lord, only makest me dwell in safety.[u]

DIRECTIONS FOR MIDNIGHT.

If you chance to wake in the night, or cannot sleep, beware, Philotheus, of idle and unclean thoughts, which will then be apt to crowd into your mind, and therefore to arm yourself against them, I advise you to learn the 130th and the 139th Psalms by heart, or treasure up some ejaculations in your mind, which will be excellent matter for your thoughts to feed on. For instance:

[u] Psalm iv. 9.

EJACULATIONS FOR THE NIGHT.

Thou, Lord, hast granted Thy lovingkindness in the day time, and in the night season will I sing of Thee, and make my prayer to the God of my life.[v]

O Lord, the holy angels are now before Thy throne in heaven, they never rest day or night from thy praises, and with them do I now sing hallelujah, salvation, and honour, and glory, and power, be unto our God, for ever and ever. Amen, Amen.[w]

Lord, I know Thou wilt one day call me to give an account of my stewardship, but when Thou wilt come I know not, whether at even, or at midnight, or at cock-crowing, or in morning.[x]

O do Thou give me grace to watch, and to pray always, that at Thy coming Thou mayest say to me, "Well done, good and faithful servant, enter into the joy of thy Master. Amen, blessed Lord, Amen.

[v] Psalm xiii. 10.　[w] Rev. vii. 15.　[x] Mark xiii. 35.

But have a care, Philotheus, you fix not
your mind too much, neither strive to repeat
too many devout expressions, for fear of
hindering your sleep, and of indisposing
yourself for the duties of the day following.

DIRECTIONS FOR THE LORD'S DAY.

A good Christian, Philotheus, that takes
care to spend every day well, will take more
than ordinary care to sanctify the Lord's
Day, it being the proper employment of
that day to attend God's worship, and to
provide for our souls, and therefore it is fit
you should add some petitions to your
morning and evening prayer, relating to the
solemn duties of the day; such as these are
which follow.

BEFORE CHURCH TIME.

O my God, I humbly beseech Thee to
prepare my soul to worship Thee this day
acceptably, with reverence and godly fear;
fill me with that faith which works by love;

purify my heart from all vain, or worldly,
or sinful thoughts; fix my affections on
things above all the day long, and, O Lord,
give me grace to receive Thy word, which
I shall hear this day, into an honest and
good heart, and to bring forth fruit with
patience.ʸ Hear me, O God, for the sake
of Jesus my Saviour, Amen, Amen.

When you come into the church or
chapel, not only on the Lord's Day, but on
any other day, use this short preparatory
prayer at your first kneeling down.

IN THE CHURCH.

O Lord, I humbly beg Thy Holy Spirit
to help my infirmities at this time, and to
dispose my heart to devotion, that my prayers
and praises may be acceptable in Thy sight,
through Jesus Christ my Saviour. Amen.

AFTER CHURCH TIME.

Glory be to Thee, O Lord God Almighty,
glory be to Thee, Who hast permitted me to

ʸ Luke viii. 15.

appear before Thee this day, and to tread Thy courts!

Lord, pardon all my failings in Thy service this day past, the wanderings and coldness, and indevotion of my prayers. For the sake of my blessed Saviour, have mercy upon me.

Lord, make me a doer of Thy word, and not a hearer only, lest I deceive my own soul[z].

When you are called to repetition at night, remember, Philotheus, to make some amends for your negligent hearing at the church, and treasure up in your memory some little portion of those instructions you have heard, to direct your practice.

DIRECTIONS FOR RECEIVING THE HOLY EUCHARIST.

The receiving of the blessed sacrament, good Philotheus, is the most divine and solemn act of all our religion, and it ought

z James i 22.

to be the zealous endeavour of every true Christian, by God's assistance, to prepare his soul with the most serious and most devout dispositions he possibly can to approach the holy altar: you are therefore to consider what you are to do before receiving, what in the time of receiving, and what after receiving.

Before Receiving.

The duties you are to perform before receiving, are all comprehended in that one rule which St. Paul gives us,[a] "Let a man examine himself, and so let him eat of that bread and drink of that cup," which are in a manner commented on by the Church, in the exhortation before the sacrament, which I advise you to read over in your Common-prayer book.

To put this rule in practice, it is your best way, Philotheus, at some convenient time to withdraw yourself into your chamber, or into the chapel, and there to begin to

a : Cor. xi 28.

commune with your own heart, and to call your sins to remembrance; but first pray heartily to God for His grace to assist you.

Prayer before Examination.

Hear the voice of my humble petition, O Lord, now I cry unto Thee, and lift up my hands toward Thy mercyseat.

Behold, Lord, now I am about to search into my own heart; but alas, alas! my heart is deceitful, and desperately wicked, how can I know it?[b] Thou therefore that searchest the heart, and triest the reins, discover to me all the evil and deceits of my own heart, that I may confess, and bewail, and forsake them, and obtain mercy. Lord, hear me, Lord, help me, for the merits of Jesus my Saviour. Amen, Amen.

Rules to be observed in Examination.

Having prayed for God's assistance, doubt not, Philotheus, but He will vouchsafe it you;

b 2 Jer. xvii. 9.

and to guide you in your examination the better, observe these following directions:

When you examine yourself, either by the following catalogue, or by that in the Whole Duty of Man, or by any other, pause a while on every particular; and if you find yourself not guilty, then say, Glory be to Thee, O Lord, for preserving me from this sin; and so go on.

When your conscience answers guilty, then it will be your best way, having said, Lord, have mercy upon me, and forgive me this sin, to write down that sin in a paper, that you may have it ready to confess to God, when your examination is done.

You are to consider, Philotheus, that there are several degrees of young penitents, and some are more, some less sinful. For instance,

Some there are, who either through want of conscientious parents, or through often stifling good motions, or through inconstancy, or heedlessness, or unadvisedness, or vicious company, or ill nature, or youthful lusts,

and the like, have been from their infancy
very negligent of learning, or at least of
practising their duty.

Again, some there are amongst these,
whose sins are more heinous than ordinary,
in regard they are accompanied with several
aggravations : for any sin is much aggravated,
if it be committed knowingly, or deliberately,
or frequently : and more than that, if it be
committed obstinately, or presumptuously, or
on slight, or no temptations, or against checks
of conscience, or against reproofs, or admoni-
tions, or chastisements, or vows to the con-
trary; but most of all, if it be committed
so long, and so often, till it becomes habitual,
till the sinner does take delight in it, or
boast of it, or makes a mock at it, or tempts
others also to commit it. All these and the
like circumstances do very much heighten
the guilt of any sins.

You may easily from hence guess what
progress you have made in wickedness, and
if you find yourself in the number of any of
these, by all means, good Philotheus, resolve

to repent immediately, and to confess your sins with all their aggravations; for be sure of this, that every other step you run farther from Heaven, every other hour you continue longer in a sinful course, makes your sins the more hard to be mastered, and your repentance the more difficult.

On the other side, some there are, though I fear but few, who having been brought up in the nurture and admonition of the Lord, have been by the goodness of God, secured from violent temptations, and enormous sins, who have, like Josiah, while they were yet young, sought the Lord, and have in a great measure kept their baptismal vow, and preserved a sense of their duty.[e]

Such as these have fewer sins to confess, and those sins less aggravated, and therefore have greater obligations to magnify God's mercy than others: but if you are in this number, have a care of growing careless in your examination, or of presuming on your own innocence: for if we say, or think we

e 2 Chron. xxxiv. 3.

have no sin, we miserably deceive ourselves. [d]

O Philotheus, the best of men, God knows,
have very much evil in them to detest and
bewail, and have infinite need of a Saviour,
and therefore let him that standeth, take
heed lest he fall. [e]

Whatever you do then, be sure to keep
your heart with all diligence, and pray for
constant supplies of God's grace, for perhaps
the devil defers his tempting you till you
are grown up, and become your own master,
and have not that tenderness of offending,
or that awe of parents, or superiors, which
you now have.

Be not over-scrupulous, Philotheus, either
to make yourself guilty of more sins than
really you are, or to reckon up all your
infirmities, or daily failings, or sins of omission,
which would render your examination endless
and impossible; but examine yourself chiefly
about your wilful sins, or sins of commission;
and know, there be many sins, even of

d 1 John 1. 8.   e 1 Cor. x. 12.

commission, that you may doubt whether you have committed or no; many that you have quite forgot; but be not disheartened at it, for holy David hath taught you, that a general confession for such sins is enough, when he prays to God to cleanse him from his secret faults.f

That you may gain a true sense of your sins by your examination, labour to imprint in your mind awful apprehensions of the day of judgment, and of God the great Judge, in Whose presence you now are; and to raise such apprehensions, dwell a while in such meditations as these.

MOTIVES TO EXAMINATION.

O my soul, thou art now in the presence of the great Judge of Heaven and earth, before whose dreadful tribunal thou must certainly appear at the day of judgment, to give a strict account of all thy actions, and every idle word, of every evil thought, and thy own conscience will then be thy accuser.

f Psalm xix. 12.

Think, O my soul, think, if thou canst, what unimaginable horrors will seize an impenitent sinner, when the last trump calls him out of the grave, and the devils begin to drag him to God's judgment-seat! What would such a wretch give to purchase one such opportunity of repentance, as God now in great mercy gives thee? If ever thou hopest to escape those horrors, O my soul, make thy peace with God, judge thyself here, lest thou be condemned hereafter.

THE EXAMINATION ITSELF.

I adjure thee, O my soul, in the presence of the great Judge, who knows all the secrets of thy heart, I adjure thee, as thou wilt answer before God's judgment-seat at the last day, to tell me;

Does not thy daily experience teach thee, that thy whole nature is corrupt, pron to all that is evil, averse to all that is good?

How hast thou spent thy time, from thy childhood to this very moment?

How hast thou kept the solemn vow of thy baptism?

What good duties hast thou omitted?

What sins hast thou committed?

In particular, what sin art thou guilty of, more immediately against God?

Art thou guilty of any infidelity or atheism, any distrust in, or presumption on, or despair of God's mercy?

Art thou guilty of any wilful ignorance of God, or of any idolatry, in worshipping any creature? Hast thou loved any thing more than God, or feared any one above Him?

Hast thou been guilty of hypocrisy in God's service, or of forsaking God, and of resorting to the devil, to witches or wizards?

Art thou guilty of repining or murmuring at God's providence, or of being impatient under His afflictions, or of being unthankful for His mercies, or of being disobedient to His commands, or of being incorrigible under His judgments?

When, and in what manner hast thou been guilty of dishonouring God?

By blasphemous or irreligious thoughts or discourses; or by tamely hearing others blaspheme?

By taking God's most holy name in vain, or by customary or false swearing, or by the breach of any lawful oath or solemn vows?

By any sacrilege or irreverent behaviour in God's house, or misspending the Lord's day, or any neglect of or inattention to God's word read or preached, or unprofitableness under the means of grace?

Have I dishonoured God, by coldness, and wanderings, and indevotion, or carelessness in my prayers, or by any weariness in his service, or by any total neglect of it, or by unworthy communicating?

By impenitence, or putting off the evil day, or superficial and partial repentances, or frequent relapses, or resisting the good motions of God's Spirit?

By abetting any schism, or heresy, or profaneness?

O my soul, what sins art thou guilty of, more immediately against thyself?

Art thou guilty of pride, either of thy clothes, or of thy estate, or of thy credit, or of thy parts, or of thy own holiness, or of boasting of thy own good deeds, or of commending thyself, or of being greedy of praise, or of performing good duties to gain applause, or of committing sin to avoid reproach of men?

Hast thou been immoderately greedy of riches, or of sensual pleasures, or guilty of peevishness or of too violent, or too lasting fits of anger, or of inconstancy, or of inconsideration, or of discontentedness with any condition?

Hast thou been guilty of misspending thy time, or of negligence in resisting temptations, or of not improving those opportunities of learning and piety which God gives thee in this place, or of abusing thy natural parts to sin?

Hast thou been guilty of any intemperance in eating, or in drinking, or in sleeping, or in recreations, spending too much time on them, or being too greedy after them?

Hast thou been guilty of idleness, or of downright drunkenness, or of laughing at it in others?

Hast thou been guilty of any uncleanness in the eye, or of the hand, or of the fancy, of any lasciviousness, or lust, or fornication, or adultery; or hast thou taken delight in lewd company, or in vicious or unchaste songs, or stories, or expressions?

O my soul, what sins art thou guilty of, more immediately against thy neighbour?

How, when, where, against whom hast thou been guilty of any injury, or injustice, or oppression, or breach of trust, or promise, or of any fraud, or theft, or flattery, or dissimulation, or treachery, or lying, or of giving any just scandal?

How, when, where, against whom hast thou been guilty of any ill language, or detraction, or slander, or tale-bearing, or rash censuring, or backbiting, or of contemning, or scoffing at thy neighbour, either for his infirmities, or for his being religious?

How, when, where, against whom hast thou been guilty of any contentiousness, or spite, or revenge, or of delighting causelessly to grieve thy neighbour, or of railing, or of actually hurting him, or of murdering him in thy mind, by ill wishes or curses? Hast thou been guilty of bitter imprecations, or bearing false witness, or covetousness of any thing he possesses?

Hast thou been guilty of unthankfulness to those that have done thee good, or have reproved thee, or of uncharitableness to the poor, or to any Christian in distress, or of any unnaturalness to any of thy relations, or of any evil speaking, or disrespect, or stubbornness against any of thy governors either civil or ecclesiastical; or in particular against thy parents or superiors in this place, or of any wilful disobedience to the lawful commands of all, or either of them?

Hast thou tempted any other to sin, by connivance, or encouragement, or command, or persuasion, and mightily increased thy own guilt, by furthering the damnation of thy brother ?

In case, Philotheus, you do find this examination too difficult for you, or are afraid you shall not rightly perform it, or meet with any scruples or troubles of conscience in the practice of it, I then advise you, as the church does, to go to one of your superiors in this place, to be your spiritual guide, and be not ashamed to unburden your soul freely to him, that besides his ghostly counsel, you may receive the benefit of absolution: for though confession of our sins to God is only matter of duty, and absolutely necessary, yet confession to our spiritual guide also, is by many devout souls found to be very advantageous to true repentance.

If upon your examination, Philotheus, you find you have any way wronged your neighbour, resolve upon the first opportunity to make him some suitable satisfaction, and to ask his forgiveness; for you are first to

be reconciled to your brother, before you
come to the altar to offer your gifts.

If you are guilty of tempting any other
to sin, ask God's pardon for him, as well as
for yourself, and, if you have any opportunity
to do it, exhort him to repentance.

But if any have wronged you, forgive the
injury presently; for you beg forgiveness of
God on this very condition, that you yourself
forgive your brother.

This examination of yourself, Philotheus,
I suppose will be task enough for you at
one time; and therefore that you may not
tire yourself, you may conclude with this short
prayer.

A PRAYER AFTER EXAMINATION.

O Lord God, I have now, by Thy assist-
ance, considered my own evil ways: O
Thou Who only knowest the heart, and
Who only canst change it, create in me such

g Matt. v. 23, 24.

a broken and contrite heart which Thou hast promised not to despise, and so deep a sense of my own sin and misery, that my repentance may bear some proportion to my guilt. O my God, pardon all my failings, and perfect that good work Thou hast begun in me, for the merits of Jesus my Saviour, in Whose holy words I sum up all my wants. Our Father, &c.

At the very next opportunity of retiring you can get, resolve, good Philotheus, with the prodigal, to return to your heavenly Father, and humbly to beg forgiveness; and having brought your catalogue of sins with you, kneel down, and with the lowest prostration of soul and body, make your confession to God of your sins, and of their aggravations.

A FORM OF CONFESSION.

O Thou great Judge of heaven and earth, before Whose glorious Majesty, even the good angels, who never sinned, fall prostrate and tremble.

With what debasement and dread ought I to appear before Thy awful presence, who am but dust and ashes, and, which is infinitely worse, a miserable wretched sinner!

Holy, holy, holy, Lord God Almighty, Thou art of purer eyes than to behold evil with the least approbation; the way of the wicked, and the sacrifice of the wicked is an abomination to Thee![h]

Woe is me then, O Lord, woe is me, for I have inclined unto wickedness with my heart, but for the sake of Thy well-beloved Son, cast not out my prayer nor turn Thy mercy from me.[i]

Miserable wretch that I am, I have gone astray from the very womb; I was shapen in wickedness, and in sin did my mother conceive me! Who can bring a clean thing out of an unclean? What is man then, O God, that he should be clean; or he that is born of a woman, that he should be righteous!

h Prov. xv. 8.   i Psalm lxvi. 20.

Thou, Lord, puttest no trust in Thy saints, and the heavens are not clean in Thy sight, and the very angels Thou chargest with folly ! [k]

How much more abominable then, and filthy am I, who daily drink iniquity like water !

Lord, pity and cleanse, and forgive and save me, for Thy mercies' sake.

I know, O God, that in my flesh dwelleth no good thing; for when I would do good, evil is present with me, and I see a law in my members warring against the law of my mind, and bringing me into captivity to the law of sin. [l]

Lord, have mercy upon me, and deliver me from this body of death, from this tyranny of sin.

Alas, alas, my whole nature is corrupt, infinitely prone to all evil, and averse to all that is good; my understanding is full of ignorance and error; my will is perverse, my memory tenacious of all things that may

[k] Job iv. 18. [l] Rom. vii. 23.

pollute me, and forgetful of my duty; my passions are inordinate, my senses the inlets of all impurity, and I have abused all my faculties; I am unclean, unclean!

Lord, pity and cleanse, and forgive and save me, for Thy mercies' sake.

O Lord God, how have I through my whole life violated the solemn vow I made to Thee in my baptism, by eagerly pursuing the vanities of this wicked world, by easily yielding to the temptations of the devil, by greedily indulging my own carnal desires and lusts, by a fruitless and dead faith, and by disobedience to Thy holy will and commands.

Father, I have sinned against Heaven, and in Thy sight, and am no more worthy to be called Thy son.

I have sinned, O Lord God, I have sinned against Thee, by—

Here confess out of your paper, the sins which you have committed more immediately against God, with their aggravations that accompany them. For instance:

Lord, I have committed this sin, or these sins frequently, against checks of conscience, &c. *and then add:*

Father, I have sinned against Heaven, and in Thy sight, and am no more worthy to be called Thy son. O pity, and cleanse, and forgive, and save me for Thy mercies' sake.

I have sinned, O Lord God, I have sinned against Thee, and against my own self, by—

Here confess the sins you have committed more immediately against yourself, with their aggravations, &c. and say as before:

Father, I have sinned against Heaven, &c.
I have sinned, O Lord God, I have sinned against Thee, and against my neighbour, by—

Here confess the sins you have committed more immediately against your neighbour, with their aggravations, &c, and as before:

Father, I have sinned against Heaven, &c.
O Lord God, my wickedness is great and my iniquities are infinite; they are more in

number than the hairs of my head, and my heart would fail me, but that I well know Thy mercies are more numberless than my sins.[m]

Have mercy upon me therefore, O Lord, according to Thy great goodness, according to the multitude of Thy mercies do away my offences.[n]

Who, alas, can tell how oft he offendeth! O cleanse Thou me from my secret faults, from all my sins of ignorance, or infirmity, or omission, or which I have not observed, or which I have forgot, Lord, lay none of them to my charge; Father, forgive me; Lord Jesus, have mercy upon me.

O remember not the sins and offences of my youth, but receive me, O heavenly Father, into the arms of Thy Fatherly compassion, as Thou didst the returning prodigal, and forgive me all my transgressions, for the merits of Jesus, Thy only well-beloved Son, and my Saviour.   Amen, Amen.

m Psalm xl. 12.   n Psalm li. 1.

When you have thus confessed your sins, good Philotheus, endeavour to be still more sensible of them, and to bewail them with a true penitential hatred, and shame, and sorrow for them; then make steady resolutions of forsaking them, and cry earnestly to God for pardon and grace; for you must as well put on the new man, as put off the old.o   Of all which acts of repentance, I give you the following instances, and advise you to say them over as devoutly as possibly you can.

Acts of Shame.

O Lord God, I am ashamed, and blush to lift up my face to Thee, for my iniquities are increased over my head, and my trespasses are grown up unto the heavens.p

O my soul, what fruit have I reaped from all the pleasures of sin which flattered me, which are but vanity and vexation of spirit!

Lord, I am ashamed of my own folly and madness, and disingenuity, when I call to

o Eph. iv. 21.   p Ezra ix. 6.

mind how greedily I have sucked in my own pollution; how treacherously I have betrayed my own soul to temptations, and combined with the very devils, to hasten and increase my own damnation; how obstinately I have fled from Thee, when Thy mercy pursued me with promises of pardon; how unworthily I have abused Thy goodness and forbearance, and long suffering, which should have led me to repentance.

Surely after I was turned I repented; and since I have considered my ways, I am ashamed; yea, even confounded, because I bear the reproach of my youth.q

Acts of Abhorrence.

I hate all evil ways, O Lord, but Thy law will I love.r

O Lord God, nothing is more abominable in Thy sight, or more diabolical; nothing more defaces Thy Divine Image, or makes me more odious in Thy purest eyes, than sin: and therefore I hate and abhor it!

q Jer. xxxi. 19.   r Psalm cxix. 13.

O Lord God, I confess I have nothing good in me, nothing that can any way move Thee to compassionate so loathsome a sinner, but Thy own free, and undeserved, and infinite mercy, and the merits of my Saviour!

O Lord God, I cannot but admire the riches of Thy goodness, who hast spared me so long, and hast given me this opportunity of repentance. O do Thou yet magnify Thy mercy more in my forgiveness. O cleanse me from all that filth my soul hath contracted, which now renders me odious to my own self, as well as to Thee.

Acts of Contrition.

Miserable wretch that I am, that I should begin so early to offend my Creator, and sin so much in so short time!

Lord, I fear I never yet throughly considered how evil, and how bitter a thing it is to depart from Thee, O make me every day more and more sensible of the error of my ways, and of my own infinite vileness!

Miserable wretch that I am, that ever I

should commit those sins, which expose me to all the vials of Thy wrath, to all the curses of Thy law, to all Thy judgments temporal or spiritual, in this life, and to all the horrors and despair, and torments of the damned in the life to come!

Miserable wretch that I am, that ever I should transgress that law of Thine, O God, which is so just and holy, and good and perfect, and so condescending to my infirmities; and in keeping of which there are so great, so unconceivable rewards!

O that with Mary Magdalen I could weep much and love much, having so much to be forgiven!ˢ

O gracious Lord, look on me, as Thou didst on Peter, and let Thy compassionate look so pierce my heart, that I may weep bitterly for my sins! ᵗ

O Lord God, break this hard heart, for Thou only canst do it, and melt it into tears of contrition! Miserable wretch that I am, that I should sin so much, and yet grieve so little!

s Luke vii. 39.   t Luke xxii. 61.

Woe is me, miserable wretch, woe is me, that ever I should offend so indulgent, so liberal, so tender a Father!

Woe is me, that ever I should repay the infinite love, and the intolerable sufferings of my Saviour for me, with nothing but those sins which occasioned those very sufferings.

Woe is me, that ever I should grieve the Holy Spirit, by rejecting of many of His good motions, from Whom only I derive grace and consolation?

O Lord God, every slight worldly trouble is apt to draw back plenty of tears from mine eyes, but when I would weep for my sins, which are the greatest calamities that can possibly befall me, either my eyes are dry, or my tears too few, to bewail so many provocations!

O blessed Spirit, instil true penitent sorrow into my soul, make my head waters, and my eyes fountains of tears, or do Thou supply the want of them with sighs and groans unutterable![u]

u Romans viii. 26.

But alas, I know all the tears I can possibly shed, can never wash away the least of my sins; it is Thy blood only, Lord, that can do it!

O blessed Saviour, how can I ever sufficiently lament the guilt of my sins, which was so great, that nothing but Thy own inestimable blood could expiate!

O heavenly Father, in the defect of my own tears, I offer Thee the blood of Thy own well-beloved Son, for His sake have mercy upon me.   Amen, Amen,

Resolution.

O Lord God, with shame I confess that other lords besides Thee have hitherto had dominion over me.[x]

I have been in the snare of the devil, and have been led captive by him, and sin hath reigned in my mortal body, and I have obeyed it in the lusts thereof; but henceforth I resolve to serve none but Thee, and from this very moment I utterly forsake all my sins, and turn to Thee.[y]

x Isai. xxvi. 13.   y 2 Tim. ii. 26.; Rom. vi. 2.

O my God, I do from my heart renew my baptismal vow, which, alas, I have hitherto so often violated! I do for ever renounce the devil and all his works, and all his temptations! I do for ever renounce all the vanities of this wicked world, which may prevent me from Thy service, and all the sinful lusts of the flesh!

O my God, I do steadfastly believe all the articles of the Christian faith, and I will keep Thy holy will and commandments, and walk in the same all the days of my life!

All this I am bound to do and believe, and by Thy help so I will; and I heartily thank Thee, O heavenly Father, who hast called me to this state of salvation, through Jesus Christ my Saviour; and I humbly pray Thee for His sake to give me grace, that I may continue in the same to my life's end.

Oblation.

Blessed be Thy name, O Lord God, who

hast set before me life and death, and hast bid me choose life.

Behold, Lord, I do with all my heart choose life, I choose Thee, O my God, for Thou art my life.

Save, Lord, and hear me, O King of heaven, and accept my sacrifice, even the sacrifice of my whole heart which I now give Thee.

O my God, I offer Thee my senses and passions, and all my faculties; I offer Thee all my desires, all my designs, all my studies, all my endeavours, all the remainder of my life; all that I have, or am, I offer up all entirely to Thy service.

Lord, sanctify me wholly, that my whole spirit, soul and body, may become Thy temple. O do Thou dwell in me, and be Thou my God, and I will be Thy servant.[s] Amen, Amen.

Acts of Charity.

O Lord God, I do from henceforth resolve to love my neighbour as myself, and

s 1 Cor. vi 19.

to love Him not in word only, but in deed and in truth.[a]

I do from my heart forgive all men their tresspasses, do Thou, Lord, forgive them also.

Lord, bless them that hate me, and do good to them that have any way despitefully used me, O repay them good for evil.

O my God, bless all those that I have any way wronged; have mercy on all those to whose sins I have been any way accessary, and give them all grace to forgive me. Amen, Amen.

Petition for Pardon.

O Thou Father of mercies, and God of all consolation, be merciful to me a miserable sinner!

Lord, remember all Thy gracious calls of sinners to repentance, all Thy protestations, that Thou delightest not in the death of him that dies, and that Thou wouldst have all to be saved.[b]

a 1 John iii. 18.   b Ezra xviii. 32., 1 Tim. ii 4.

Lord, remember all the exceeding great and precious promises which Thou hast made to penitent sinners.

Lord, remember that Thy mercy is over all Thy works, that in mercy Thou delightest, and that all the holy angels seeing Thee well pleased in the exercise of that mercy, rejoice at the conversion of a sinner, that the greater my sins are, the more will that mercy be magnified in my forgiveness. c

Lord, remember that Thou didst so love the world, as to give Thy only beloved Son a ransom for it. d

O heavenly Father, Thou that sparedst not Thy only Son, but deliveredst Him for us, wilt Thou not with Him also freely give us all things, and if all things, wilt Thou not also give us the pardon of our sins?

O my God, I firmly believe Thou wilt; on that ransom my Saviour hath paid for me, and on all Thy gracious promises of pardon, which for His sake Thou hast made to me, I wholly rely; here only is the sure

c Luke xv. 10.   d John iii. 16.; Rom. viii.32.

and steadfast anchor of my soul, to which my faith and hope shall for ever adhere.

All this, Lord, do I plead, to implore Thy forgiveness.

Behold, Lord, though my failings are many, yet to the utmost of my power I have confessed, and bewailed, and forsaken my transgressions. Behold, Lord, I come at Thy call, and I come weary and heavy laden with the burden of my sins, be it unto me according to Thy word. O Thou that art faithful and just, forgive me my sins, and cleanse me from all unrighteousness. Lord, do Thou in no wise cast me from Thee, but heal my backslidings, and love me freely, ease me of my burden, that I may find rest in Thee, and say unto my soul, be of good cheer, thy sins are forgiven thee.[e]

O heavenly Father, for Thine own infinite mercies' sake, for Thy truth and promise sake, for all the merits and sufferings of the Son of Thy love, in whom Thou art always

e Matt. xl. 29.; 1 John l. 9.; John vi. 37.; Hosea xlv. 4.

well pleased, pardon all my sins and failings, and receive me into Thy favour. Amen, O Lord God, Amen, Amen.

A PETITION FOR GRACE IN GENERAL.

O Lord God, I have sworn, and I will perform it, that I will keep Thy righteous judgments.*f*

But, alas! I am able of myself to do nothing that is good, not so much as to think one good thought: and I no sooner shall rise from my knees, but I fear I shall be tempted to those very sins I have now so solemnly renounced, and those temptations will certainly overcome me, unless Thou, Lord, dost seasonably interpose Thy grace to withhold me.

But I can do all things through Thee strengthening me: do Thou then, O blessed Saviour, perfect Thy strength in my weakness, for in Thee only is my trust.*g*

f Psalm cxix. 106.   g Phil. ix. 13.

O my God, Thou hast promised to give
Thy Holy Spirit to those that ask it. [h]
Behold, Lord, I do humbly, I do earnestly
ask Thy Holy Spirit now of Thee, O fulfil
Thy gracious promise to me, O vouchsafe
me that Holy Spirit I pray for, to purify
my corrupt nature, to strengthen my weakness,
to comfort me in troubles, to support me
in discouragements, to succour me in temptations, and to assist me in all parts of my
duty, that I may ever hereafter live in Thy
fear, and in constant, sincere, and universal
obedience to all Thy righteous laws.

Thou, O Searcher of hearts, knowest the
sin (or sins) I am most inclined to [*here name
it, or them*], and herein will lie my greatest
danger of backsliding: but, O my God, I
beg a double portion of Thy invisible aid
against it, (*or them.*) Hold Thou up my
goings in Thy paths, that my footsteps slip
not; O work in me that victorious faith,
by which I may overcome the world, the
devil, and my own corrupt nature. [i]

h Luke xi. 13.   i 1 John v. 4.

F

True it is, O Lord God, that there are many sins which upon examination, I find, through Thy grace, I have not yet committed, and therefore not unto me, Lord, but to Thy name be the glory; but, alas! there is in my corrupt nature so great a proneness to evil, so great a curiosity to try what sin is, that without Thy restraining grace, every temptation when I shall have more age and liberty, and opportunity to enforce it, will be apt to draw me from my obedience, and to overthrow all my present resolutions.

But my help standeth in Thee, O great Creator, Who hast made heaven and earth, and I commit my soul to Thy keeping, O Thou that art faithful as well as Almighty, keep that safe which is committed to Thy trust, watch over me that I may not be beguiled by the deceitfulness of sin, or betrayed by my own treacherous heart, or surprised by my ghostly enemies; and give me grace to watch and to pray incessantly myself, lest I enter into temptation. Hear, Lord, from heaven, and succour me for

the alone merits of Jesus my Saviour.ʲ
Amen, Amen.

PETITIONS FOR PARTICULAR GRACES.

O that my ways, Lord, were made so
direct, that I might keep Thy statutes, for
then shall I not be confounded, when I have
respect unto all Thy commandments.ᵏ

Vouchsafe me Thy Holy Spirit, therefore,
O Lord God, to work in me whatever is
well-pleasing in Thy sight, that for the time
to come I may bring forth fruits meet for
repentance.

O let it be Thy good pleasure to create
in me a saving knowledge of Thee, and of
my duty, justifying faith, true sanctifying
grace, and a purifying hope, an ardent love,
and a filial fear of Thee, a constant desire
of pleasing Thee, and a great tenderness of
offending Thee!

Lord, create in me a penitent heart, a
resigned will, and mortified affections, an

ʲ 1 Peter iv. 19.　　　　ᵏ Psalm cxix.

habitual mindfulness of Thy presence, and a steady devotion in my prayers, sincere intentions, and zeal for Thy glory, perseverance in all holy purposes, and constancy in all trials and temptations.

Lord, create in me a reverential awe of Thy name, a delight in Thy service, a secret regard to this day and house of prayer, and a great attention to Thy word ; a daily care of my time, and diligence in my studies.

Lord, make me chaste and temperate, humble and advisable, and patient of reproof; and create in me a cheerful and meek, a contented and considerate, a quiet and peaceful spirit.

Lord, bless me with health, and competency of living, with a good understanding, a retentive memory, and a ready apprehension ; and with such a measure of temporal good things, as Thou seest fit for me, and give me grace to make a right use of all those blessings I have already received.

Lord, purify my thoughts, bridle my tongue, guide all my actions, guard all my senses, stop my ears, and turn away my eyes from sin and vanity.

Lord give me grace to be just in all my dealings, to do to all men as I would they should do to me, to be subject to my parents, and to all my superiors, to the king as supreme, and to all civil magistrates, to the pastors of Thy church, and to all my governors in this place: O grant that I may tender due honour and obedience to them all in their several stations.

Lord, make me willing to forgive injuries, and unwilling to offer any; make me grateful to my benefactors, friendly to my equals, condescending to my inferiors, compassionate to the afflicted, charitable to the poor according to my ability, a lover of good men, and kind to my enemies, and give me grace to keep always a conscience void of offence towards Thee, and towards men, and to continue in the communion of the church without wavering.

O merciful God, keep Thy servant from all wilful, deliberate, or presumptuous sins, and let no wickedness have dominion over me.

From stubbornness and pride, idleness and
sloth, intemperance and youthful lusts, inconstancy and lying, good Lord deliver me!

From irreligious principles and false teachers,
unruly passions and violent temptations, from
contracting vicious habits, or taking pleasure
in sin, from profaneness and ill company, envy
and malice, detraction and uncharitableness,
good Lord deliver me!

From the errors and vices of the age, and
all remanent affections to sin, from the sin
(or sins) my corrupt nature is most inclined to
[*here name it or them*]; from whatsoever is
offensive to Thee, or destructive to my own
soul, good Lord deliver me!

Hear me, O heavenly Father, and conform
my whole life to the example of my blessed
Saviour, and that for His sake, in whose holy
words I sum up all my wants. Our Father
which art in heaven, &c.

You have now, good Philotheus, by God's
help, gone over the hardest part of your preparation for the Holy Sacrament; the next

thing you are to do, is to examine yourself,
whether you do sufficiently understand what the
sacrament is, then to ask yourself with what
intentions you do approach it, and to pray for
God's grace to dispose you for worthily receiving, and all these particulars, together with
all that you are to know and believe concerning
the blessed sacrament, are contained in these
following meditations, which I advise you to
read over devoutly at several times, till you are
in some measure affected with them.

MEDITATIONS ON THE HOLY EUCHARIST.

On the outward Elements.

I adore Thee, O blessed Jesus, my Lord,
and my God, when I consider what that sacrament is, to which Thou now invitest me, and
of what parts it consists; of an outward and
visible sign, and of an inward and spiritual
grace! For Thou, Lord, who knowest our
infirmities, and how little able we are to conceive things heavenly and spiritual, in pity to
our dark and feeble apprehensions, hast or-

dained outward, and obvious, and visible signs
to represent to our minds Thy grace which is
inward and invisible; Thou hast ordained bread
and wine, which is our corporeal food, to pic-
ture out to our faith the food of our souls.

On the Inward Part or Thing signified.

I know, O my God, that I must look
through the outward elements and fix my faith
on that which they signify, and which is the
inward and invisible grace, even Thy own blessed Body and Blood, which is verily and indeed
taken and received by the faithful in the Lord's
supper.

But tell me, O thou whom my soul loveth,
how canst Thou give us Thy flesh to eat!

Lord, Thou hast told me that Thy words,
they are spirit and they are life, and are therefore not carnally to be understood; Lord, I
believe, help Thou my unbelief[1].

I believe Thy body and blood to be as really
present in the Holy Sacrament as Thy divine

1 John vi. 63.

power can make it, though the manner of Thy mysterious presence I cannot comprehend.

Lord, I believe that the bread that we break, and the cup that we drink, are not bare signs only, but the real communication of Thy Body and Thy Blood, and pledges to assure me of it; and I verily believe that with due preparation I come to the altar, as certainly as I receive the outward signs, so certainly shall I receive the thing signified, even Thy most blessed body and blood; to receive which inestimable blessings, O merciful Lord, do Thou fit and prepare me [m]. Amen, Amen.

Who instituted it ?

I adore Thee, O blessed Jesus, my Lord, my God, when I consider that this Holy Sacrament was Thy own institution; for it was Thou, Lord, who in the night Thou wast betrayed, didst take bread, and after that the cup, and didst bless them, and give them to Thy disciples. O blessed Saviour, let Thy Divinity thus stamped on it strike into my soul an holy

m 1 Cor. x. 16.

awe and reverence in approaching it : O create in me heavenly dispositions to celebrate so heavenly an institution ! Amen, Amen.

For what end ?

I adore Thee, O blessed Jesus, my Lord and my God, when I consider for what end Thou didst institute Thy Holy Sacrament, implied in Thy own command, Do this in remembrance of Me.

But what need this command, O gracious Lord ; is it possible for me ever to forget Thee my Saviour, who hast done so great things for me !

Alas ! alas ! my own sad experience tells me it is.   Woe is me, every temptation, every vanity, is apt to make me forget Thee, though Thy own dying words bid me remember Thee!

But, O blessed Lord, for Thy infinite mercies' sake pardon all my stupid forgetfulness and ingratitude hitherto, and do. Thou now create in me such a thankful and lively remembrance of Thy dying for me, that may excite

> to give up myself entirely to Thee, a

Thou didst give up Thyself on the cross for me. Amen, Amen.

A Thanksgiving for Christ's Suffering.

O Thou my crucified Saviour, glory be to Thee, for causing Thy sufferings to be registered in the Gospel; there I have read and remember the works and triumphs of Almighty love, for which I will always adore and praise Thee.

I remember, O gracious Lord, how Thou, who thoughtest it no robbery to be equal with God, wast made in the fashion of frail man [n], of the vilest and most contemptible of men: for Thou tookest on Thee the form of a very servant: I remember how many reproaches and contradictions, and blasphemies and persecutions, Thou didst endure from a wicked and perverse generation, and all this to save us sinful men.

O Lord Jesus, was ever sorrow like unto Thy sorrow? Worthy art Thou, O Lamb that was slain, to receive power, and riches, and wisdom,

n Phil. ii. 7.

*and strength, and honour, and glory, and
blessing°.*

I remember, O gracious Lord, how Thou
didst endure a most bitter agony, and didst
sweat great drops of blood, falling to the
ground: how Thou who art God above all,
blessed for ever, was treacherously betrayed,
and apprehended, and bound as a malefactor;
how Thou wast set at nought by Herod, and
his men of war, and forsaken of all Thy disciples, and denied by Peter, and all this to
save us sinful men.p

O Lord Jesus was ever, &c.

I remember, how Thou, O God of truth,
wast accused by false witnesses, how Thou
whom all the Angels adore, wast blindfolded
and buffeted, and mocked, and spit upon, and
stripped naked, and scourged; and all this that
we might be healed by Thy stripes, and to
save us sinful men.

O Lord Jesus, was ever, &c.

I remember, Lord, how Thou that art the

great Judge of heaven and earth, wast Thyself
dragged to the judgment-seat, and condemned;
how Thou, O King of heaven, wast crowned
with thorns, and oppressed with the weight
of Thy own cross, and all this to save us sinful
men.

O Lord Jesus was ever, &c.

I remember, O blessed Saviour, how Thou,
who art the Lord of Glory, and the sole
Author of life, wast put to a most igno-
minious death, how Thy hands and Thy
feet were nailed to a cross, how Thou wast
crucified between two thieves, and numbered
with the transgressors: how Thou hadst a
potion given Thee to imbitter Thy very
last gasp, and all this to save us sinful
men!

O Lord Jesus, was ever, &c.

I remember, O gracious Lord, how when
Thou wert hanging on the very cross, Thou
wast scoffed at and reviled; how infinitely
then Thou wert afflicted and bruised for our

transgressions, when the iniquities of us all were laid on Thy shoulders; how Thou didst then express an anguish greater than all the tortures of Thy crucifixion, when Thou didst cry out, My God, My God, why hast Thou forsaken Me? And how thou didst at the last give up the ghost, and die Thyself, that we might live?

O Lord Jesus, was ever, &c.

I unfeignedly believe, O gracious Lord, that Thou didst suffer all this for sinful men, and in particular for me, when we were all Thy utter enemies, and had nothing in us to move Thee to pity us but our extreme misery, nothing to move Thee to save us but our great unworthiness, and Thy greater mercy.

O the depth of the riches of Thy love, blessed Lord, how unutterable is Thy mercy, and Thy love past finding out!

O all ye holy Angels, behold and wonder, wretched man hath sinned against God, and

God Himself has suffered the sinner's punishment!

"Was there ever sorrow like that which my Lord and my God endured for me?"

"Was there any love like to that love my Lord and my God hath shewed me?"

O ye blessed host of heaven, who rejoice at the conversion of one single sinner. Adore and praise my crucified Saviour, who died for the sins of the world; adore and praise that unknown sorrow, that wonderful love, which you yourselves must needs admire!

O my gracious Lord, my heart is now full of the sense of Thy love, and what have I to return to Thee, but love again! 'Tis all I have to offer Thee: accept it, O merciful Lord, imperfect as it is, and do Thou daily heighten my sense of Thy love to me, that I may daily heighten my love to Thee!

O Thou infinite Lover of souls, with all my heart I love, I praise, I adore Thy love to me, but alas, I can never do it enough!

O do Thou at last, gracious Lord, translate

me to Thy kingdom of Glory, that there I may love Thee to the uttermost capacity of a creature, and praise Thee to all eternity. Amen, Lord Jesus. Amen, Amen.

What benefits we receive by it.

I adore Thee, O blessed Jesu, my Lord and my God, when I consider the benefits which through Thy mercy we receive by Thy Holy Sacrament!

Glory be to Thee, O Lord, who there makest Thy own body and blood to become our spiritual food, to strengthen and refresh our souls!

Glory be to Thee, O Lord, who by this heavenly food dost mystically unite us to Thyself; for nothing becomes one with our bodies more than the bodily food we eat which turns into our very substance, and nothing makes us become one with Thee more, than when Thou vouchsafest to become the very food of our souls!

Glory be to Thee, O Lord, who by this immortal food dost nourish our souls to

live the life of grace here, and dost raise
us up to life everlasting hereafter! Lord
do Thou evermore give me this bread! Amen,
Amen q.

Motives of receiving.

O blessed Saviour! What more powerful
motives can I have to persuade me to communicate, than Thy command, and the admirable
effects of the Holy Sacrament!

But, alas! my corrupt nature is apt to
suggest to me low and base inducements
to this duty, such as are, fear of my superiors' displeasure, if I abstain, or shame of
not appearing as devout as my equals, or the
mere custom of the place, or of the season.

But, Lord, I do from my heart renounce
all these and the like carnal considerations,
and I come to Thy altar to renew my baptismal covenant with Thee, of which Thy
sacrament is a seal.

I come to testify my sense of Thy love,

q John vi. 51.

G

O heavenly Father, in so loving the world, as to give up Thy only Son to die for me.

I come to testify my faith in Thee, and my love towards Thee, O blessed Saviour, and thankfully to commemorate Thy wonderful love in dying for me.

I come, Lord, to testify my steadfastness in the communion of Thy church, and my charity to all the world.

I come to Thy table, O Lord, out of the sense I have of the want of that spiritual food to which Thou there invitest me.

Alas, alas! I am soon apt to grow weary of welldoing. A few prayers, very little duty, is apt to tire me, every slight temptation is apt to overcome me, and I know there is no food can strengthen my soul but Thy body, no cordial can revive my drooping obedience, but Thy blood, and it is Thy most blessed body and blood I hunger and thirst after, O gracious Lord: grant that I, and all that communicate with me, may feel its saving efficacy. O feed, O refresh, O nourish our souls with it to

life everlasting, and that for Thy own infi_
nite mercy sake, which moved Thee to
offer up Thy body and blood for us! Amen,
Amen.

Prayer for preparation.

Blessed Lord Jesus! I even tremble when
I consider . that he that eateth and drinketh unworthily is guilty of Thy body and
blood, and eateth and drinketh damnation
to his own soul; and this severe sentence on
unworthy communicants makes me afraid to
come to Thy altar[r].

But when I consider that Thy sentence
is as severe against those, who being invit-
ed refuse to come, for Thou hast said,
They shall not taste of Thy supper; and
unless we eat Thy flesh, and drink Thy blood,
we have have no life in us, I am then afraid
to keep away[s].

But blessed be Thy mercy, O Lord, for
in this strait my soul is in, Thou art my guide;
Thou by giving me this opportunity of re-

[r] 1 Cor. xi. 29.   [s] John vi. 53.

ceiving, invitest me to Thy table: Thou call-
est me to seek Thy face, and my heart replies,
Thy face, Lord, will I seek!

If Thou, Lord, shouldest be extreme to
mark what is done amiss; alas! alas! I am
then unfit, not only to communicate, but to
say even my daily prayers.

I know, Lord, that if I should stay till
I am worthy to come, I should then never come;
and therefore though I am unworthy of so
unspeakable a mercy, yet I come to beg
Thy grace to make me worthy, or at least
such as Thou wilt accept!

O blessed Jesus, do Thou so open my
eye of faith to discern Thy body and blood
in the Holy Sacrament, do Thou so dispose
my soul at this time to communicate, that
I may feel all the happy effects of Thy own
Divine institution, that my soul may receive
such lasting impressions of Thy goodness,
and be so ravished with the love of Thee
and with the incomparable delights of Thy
service, and with such an early foretaste of
heaven, that all the pleasures of sin, which

in my growing years may tempt me, may appear to me tasteless and unwelcome.

O heavenly Father, clothe me with the wedding garment, even the graces of my blessed Saviour, for then am I sure to be a welcome guest to Thy table, when I shall come thither in the likeness of Thy only well-beloved Son in whom Thou art always well pleased.

O heavenly Father, fill me with a lively faith, profound humility, filial obedience, inflamed affections, and universal charity; O raise in my soul all those heavenly transports of zeal and devotion, of love and desire, of joy and delight, of praise and thanksgiving, which become the remembrance of a crucified Saviour, which become one redeemed by the blood of God, and that for His sake only that redeemed me, in whose holy words I sum up all the graces and blessings I stand in need of. Our Father which art in heaven, &c.

This prayer, Philotheus, is proper for you to add to your morning prayer, the day on which you are to receive.

DIRECTIONS IN TIME OF RECEIVING.

In time of receiving, good Philotheus, labour all you can to keep your heart affected with the public prayers, and to fill up all the vacant minutes with holy ejaculations, such as these which follow.

At going to the Altar.

In the multitude of Thy mercies, O Lord God, do I now approach Thy altar. O pardon my sins, and receive me graciously. Amen, Amen.

At the Offertory.

Blessed be Thou, O Lord God; for all things come of Thee, and of Thine own do I now give Thee[t].

O let this alms be an odour of a sweet smell, a sacrifice acceptable, and well-pleasing to Thee[u]!

t 1 Chron. xxix. 14,   u Phil. iv. 18.

At Consecrating.

O blessed Jesu, in the bread broken, I call to mind Thy body torn with whips, and thorns, and nails; and in the wine poured out, I call to mind Thy precious blood, shed for my sins!

Glory be to Thee, O Lamb of God, that didst offer Thyself a sacrifice, to take away the sins of the whole world: Lord, have mercy on me, and take away mine also.

Whilst others are communicating.

O my God, whom have I in heaven but Thee, and there is none on earth I desire, in comparison of Thee! [x]

As the hart panteth after the water-brooks, so panteth my soul after Thee, O God! [y]

My soul is a thirst for Thee, O God, my God!

Blessed Saviour, I am Thine, I am wholly Thine, for Thou hast bought me with a

x Psalm lxxiii. 25.　　　　y Psalm xlii. 1.

price, with the inestimable price of Thy own blood! ²

Lord, suffer not the price of Thy own blood to perish, and I will always glorify Thee in my body, and in my spirit which are Thine.

If there be many communicants, and Thou hast much vacant time, Philotheus, and dost want devout matter to employ Thy thoughts till all have communicated, Thou mayest then repeat the thanksgiving for Christ's sufferings, (p. 75.) either in whole, or in part, as Thou seest it needful.

When the priest cometh towards you.

O Lord God, I now desire to renew my covenant with Thee, and to seal it in this sacrament!

Lord, put Thy laws into my mind, and write them in my heart, and for the passion of Thy Son, which I now commemorate, be merciful to my unrighteousness, my sin, and iniquities remember no more, and be Thou my God, and I will be Thy servant. Amen, Amen.[a]

O. my soul, taste now, and see how gracious the Lord is![b]

After Receiving the Bread.

Glory be to Thee, O Lord, who feedest me with the bread of life.[c]

O Lord God, Who didst sanctify us by the offering of the body of Jesus once for all, sanctify me, even me, O heavenly Father.

After Receiving the Cup.

Glory be to Thee, O Lord Jesus, who permittest me to drink of the fountain of life freely!

My beloved is mine, and I am His!

Blessed Saviour, Thou hast loved us, and washed us from our sins in Thy own blood, and therefore to Thee be glory and dominion, for ever and ever. Amen, Amen.[d]

a Heb. viii 10.   b Psalm xxxiv.   c Heb. x. 10.
d Rev. i. 6.

Glory be to Thee, O Jesus my Lord, and my God, for thus feeding my soul with Thy most blessed body and blood; O let Thy heavenly food transfuse new life and new vigour into my soul, and into the souls of all that communicate with me, that our faith may daily increase, that we may all grow more humble and contrite for our sins, that we may all love Thee, and serve Thee, and delight in Thee, and praise Thee more fervently, more incessantly than ever we have done heretofore! Amen, Amen,

After the congregation is dismissed, Philotheus, if you cannot get privacy in your own chamber, I advise you at the first opportunity to go into the chapel, and there to give God thanks for that great blessing, of which He has now made you a partaker.

A Thanksgiving after Receiving.

O how plentiful is Thy goodness, my Lord and my God, which Thou hast laid up for those that fear Thee, which Thou hast laid up for those that put their trust in Thy mercy!ᵉ

Was it not love infinite enough, dearest Lord, to give Thyself for me on the cross? Was not that sacrifice of Thyself sufficient to expiate the sins of the whole world? What, Lord, couldest Thou then do more for me?

All the mighty host of heaven stood amazed to see the blood of God shed, to see their King of glory, to whom from the first moment of their being, they had sung their hallelujahs, nailed to a cross; and all this to save sinners!ᶠ

Sure, Lord, none of all those blessed spirits, with all the glorious illuminations they had, could ever have imagined how Thou couldest give Thyself more to us, than Thou hast done.

And yet for all this, Thou hast wrought new miracles of love for us, and as if it had not been love enough to have given Thyself for us on the cross, Thou hast found out a way

e Psalm xxxi. 19   f Acts xx. 28.

to give Thyself to us in the Holy Sacrament, to unite Thyself to us with the most intimate union that it is possible to conceive, to become the very food, the life, the strength, the support of my soul, to become one with me, to become the very soul of my soul!

O Lord God, this is so unconceivable a blessing, this is so Divine an union, that the very Angels, who so much desire to look into the great mystery of our redemption, who learn Thy manifold wisdom from Thy church, and frequent the places of Thy public worship, do crowd about our altar, and with awful admiration, contemplate the Holy Sacrament! g

What thanks then, gracious Lord, can I return to Thee for those wonders of love Thou hast shewed to me, wretched sinner; which the very Angels, who never sinned, so much admire?

O dearest Lord, raise Thou my devotion to the highest pitch it can possibly reach, to praise Thee; enlarge my soul to its utmost extent to love Thee!

g 1 Pet. i 12.; Eph. iii. 10 ; 1 Cor. xi. 10.

How can I evermore offend such riches of mercy, as are in Thee, O crucified Saviour! and yet whilst I carry this body of sin about me, I fear I shall! but, Lord, I do from my heart renounce and abhor all things that displease Thee, I resolve to the utmost of my power to resist all temptations, and to become as totally Thine, as my frail nature will permit me.

O gracious Lord, who hast so infinitely loved us, and given us everlasting consolation, and good hope through grace, comfort my heart, and for ever establish it, in every good word and work!

Blessing, and honour, and glory, and power, be unto Him that sitteth on the throne, and unto the Lamb for ever!

Rejoice in the Lord Jesus, O my soul, for of Him cometh my salvation.

I will love Thee, O Lord my King, and I will praise Thy name for ever and ever!

Glory be to Thee, O Lord God, for giving me this blessed opportunity of coming to Thy altar! O grant I may never more pollute my soul, which Thou hast now made Thy temple to reside in, Who art the God of purity!

Praise the Lord, O my soul: while I live will I praise the Lord; as long as I have any being I will sing praises unto Thee, O blessed Saviour, my King and my God!

O gracious Lord, pardon all my failings, accept all my prayers and praises, and supply all my wants, which I sum up in Thy own blessed words, Our Father, &c.

Remember, good Philotheus, that when you have received the Holy Sacrament, your greatest work is then but beginning, which is, to observe all the promises you have made to God of future obedience, and therefore it is good for you to read over now and then, and to renew your resolutions, and to examine yourself how you have kept them; that you may preserve in your soul a serious sense of your duty, and a conscientious care to perform it.

A FORM OF GENERAL THANKSGIVING.

" Worthy art Thou, O Lord of heaven and earth, to receive glory, and honour, and power, for Thou hast created all things, and for Thy pleasure they are and were created!" [h]

Thou hast made heaven, the heaven of heavens with all their host, the earth, and all things that are therein, Thou preservest them all, and the host of heaven praiseth Thee. [i]

Glory be to Thee, O Lord God Almighty, for creating man after Thine own image, and making so great variety of creatures to minister to his use !

Glory be to Thee, Who givest us life, and breath, and all things, Who givest us fruitful seasons, and fillest our hearts with food and gladness ! [j]

Glory be to Thee, O Lord God, for all Thy many blessings and deliverances, for all Thy forbearance and long suffering to

h Rev. iv. 11.　　i Nehem. ix. 6.　　j Acts xiv. 17.

this sinful nation; glory be to Thee, O Lord, Who hast made me also share in those public mercies, and for that light of the Gospel Thou vouchsafest us, of which the greatest part of the world is totally ignorant.

Glory be to Thee, O heavenly Father, for my being and preservation, strength and health, understanding and memory, friends and benefactors, and for all my abilities of mind and body.

Glory be to Thee, O heavenly Father, for my competent livelihood, for my education in this college, for all my known or unknown deliverances, and for the guard Thy holy Angels keep over me.

But above all, glory be to Thee for giving Thy only Son to die for my sins, and for all the spiritual blessings He has purchased for me, for my baptism, and all the opportunities Thou givest me of serving Thee, or of receiving the Holy Eucharist: for whatever sin I have escaped, for whatever good I have done, or thought, for all my helps of grace, and hopes of heaven, glory be to Thee!

Praise the Lord, O my soul, and all that is within me, praise His holy name!

Glory be to Thee, O Lord Jesus, for Thy inexpressible love to lost man! Glory be to Thee, O Lord, for condescending to take our frail nature on Thee. glory be to Thee, for all Thy heavenly doctrine to instruct us, Thy great miracles to convince us, and Thy unblameable example to guide us.

Glory be to Thee, O blessed Jesus, for Thy agony and bloody sweat, for all the torments and anguish of Thy bitter passion.

Glory be to Thee, O blessed Jesus, for Thy glorious resurrection, and ascension into heaven, and intercession for us at the right hand of Thy Father!

O gracious Lord, Thou that hast done so much for me, how can I ever sufficiently praise and love Thee!

Praise the Lord Jesus, O my soul, and all that is within me, praise His holy name!

Glory be to Thee, O blessed Spirit, glory

be to Thee for all the miraculous gifts and graces Thou didst bestow on the apostles, to fit them to convert the world, and for inspiring the sacred penmen of Holy Scripture!

Glory be to Thee for instilling holy thoughts into my soul, for all the ghostly strength, and support, and comfort, and illumination we receive from Thee; for all Thy preventing, and restraining, and sanctifying grace, glory be to Thee!

Blessed Spirit! let me never more by my sins grieve Thee, Who art the Author of life and joy to me!

Praise the Lord, O my soul, and all that is within me, praise His holy name.

Here, Philotheus, if you recite this thanksgiving on any great festival or saint's day, you may add,

Particularly, O Lord, I am bound to praise Thee, for the great blessing we this day commemorate, [*Here mention it, for instance, the Nativity of our blessed Saviour, or the like.*]

Or, for the saint, whose memory we this day

celebrate, [*Here you may name him*] and add,

Praise the Lord therefore, O my soul, and all that is within me.

Blessing, and honour, and thanksgiving, and praise, more than I can utter, more than I can conceive, be unto Thee, O most adorable Trinity, Father, Son, and Holy Ghost, by all angels, all men, all creatures, for ever and ever. Amen, Amen.

A FORM OF GENERAL INTERCESSION.

Holy, holy, holy Lord God Almighty, I, miserable sinner, humbly acknowledge that I am altogether unworthy to pray for myself; but since Thou hast commanded us to make prayers, and intercessions for all men, in obedience to Thy command, and in confidence of Thy unlimited goodness, I commend to Thy mercy and divine providence, the wants and necessities of all mankind.

Lord, let it be Thy good pleasure to restore to Thy Church catholic, primitive peace and purity, and to preserve it against the gates of hell.

Particularly, O Lord God, I implore Thy mercy for this sinful nation, for the iniquity of the land is exceeding great.

Alas, alas! we are unthankful for Thy blessings, incorrigible under Thy judgments, and unprofitable under all the means of grace, and what can we expect from Thee, but to drink deep of the cup of Thy wrath?

And, wretch that I am, my sins have increased the heap of the public impieties, and made their cry the louder to heaven for vengeance!

But, O Lord God, in the midst of judgments remember mercy; turn Thou us, Lord, and so shall we be turned: O be favourable to Thy people, and give us all grace to turn to Thee, in fasting, weeping, and mourning, to put a period to our provocations, and do Thou put a period to our punishments.

O Lord God, out of the multitude of Thy mercies, give us grace to fear Thee, and to keep Thy commandments always, that it may be well with us, and Thou mayest rejoice over us to do us good. Amen, Amen.

O let it be Thy good pleasure to bless us all, from the highest to the lowest in our several stations.

To defend the Church of England from all the assaults of schism, or heresy, or sacrilege ; and to bless all bishops, priests, and deacons, with apostolical graces, exemplary lives, and sound doctrine.

O let it be Thy great pleasure, to save and defend our sovereign lord the King, from all his enemies; grant him a long and happy reign over us ; and endue him with all those gifts and graces, which may make him a terror to evil works, and a great promoter of Thy glory.

Bless him in all his royal relations, with a great measure of all temporal good things, and with eternal glory in the world to come.

Lord, let it be Thy good pleasure to grant, To the privy council, wisdom from above. To all magistrates, integrity and zeal 'for religion.

To the gentry and commonalty, pious and just, peaceable and loyal hearts.

To our armies and navy, protection and victory.

To the whole nation, healthful, and fruitful, and peaceful times.

Lord, let it be Thy good pleasure to grant,

To all Jews, Turks, Infidels, Atheists, and Heretics, conversion.

To all malefactors, and wicked men, timely repentance.

To all holy persons, increase of grace and perseverance.

To all that I have tempted any way to sin, or with whom I have been a companion in evil, contrition and pardon.

Lord, let it be Thy good pleasure, to bless all those I have any way wronged, and to forgive those that have wronged me, to comfort the disconsolate, to give health to the sick, ease to those that are in pain, patience to the afflicted, food to the hungry, clothes to the naked, liberty to the captive, and a safe delivery to women with child.

Lord, be Thou guide to the traveller, safety

to those that are at sea, a refuge to the oppressed, be Thou a father to the fatherless, take care of widows, pity and relieve all poor prisoners for debt, and have mercy on all idiots and mad persons.

Lord, let it be Thy good pleasure to bless my parents, my brothers and sisters, and all my relations, all my friends, all my governors in this college, all my fellow scholars, all who have commended themselves to my prayers, [particularly, *here you may name them, if you see occasion*] Lord, Thou best knowest all our conditions, all our desires, all our wants. O do Thou therefore suit Thy graces and blessings to our several necessities, of body or soul!

Hear, O merciful Father, my supplications, and that for the sake of Thy Son Jesus, Who died for us all, in Whose holy words I sum up all my own, and the wants of all I pray for: Our Father which, &c.

If you are a child of the college, good Philotheus, I advise you now and then to say that usual collect, wherein you give thanks for the founder, and pray for the college; both which you have great reason to do, in private, as well as in public, when you consider that God has made the founder an instrument of doing you much good, in advantaging your education; and the blessings you pray for on the college, you have yourself a part in.

A THANKSGIVING FOR THE FOUNDER.

I give Thee humble and hearty thanks, O most merciful Father, for our founder, William of Wykham, and all other our benefactors, by whose benefits we are in this college brought up to godliness and good learning; and I beseech Thee to give us grace, so to use these Thy blessings, to the glory of Thy name, that we may become profitable members in the Church and common wealth, and may be at last partakers of the immortal glory of the resurrection, through Jesus Christ our Lord. Amen, Amen.

DIRECTIONS TO USE THE FOREGOING PRAYERS.

Have a great care, good Philotheus, that you make not any of the rules here given you, a pretence to neglect the orders and duties of the place you live in, or of the school ; for that were idleness rather than devotion.

When you fix on a day to examine your soul, or to confess your sins in, believe me, Philotheus, nothing will more enforce your prayers and repentance, than if they are accompanied with fasting and alms, as you may see in the example of Cornelius, whose prayers, and fasting, and alms, all joined together, were so acceptable to God, as made Him send, first an angel from heaven, and after the angel, an apostle, and after the apostle, the Holy Ghost, to confirm and enlighten him.[k]

But take notice, Philotheus, that all the fasting I advise you to, is only to some fasting-day, on some one Friday, or Saturday, when your commons are less than on other days, to

k Acts x.

content yourself with your bare allowance, and withal to lay aside some small matter, according to your stock, for the poor.

But beware you do not your duty only to be seen, or approved of by others, for this were hypocrisy ; and take heed your performance do not puff you up with a vain conceit of your holiness, and that you are better than your fellows, for this were abominable pride; and alas ! when you have done the best you can, you fall infinitely short of your duty, and it is God's mere mercy, not any the least worth in you, makes your service any way acceptable to Him.

When you have once throughly examined yourself, good Philotheus, and made a particular confession of the sins of your whole life, and begged pardon, there is not the same absolute necessity of such laborious examination at your next communicating, especially if you examine yourself carefully every night, and daily repent of the evil of the day past, and are not conscious to yourself of any great and notorious sins since your last confession, for if you are not, the examination and confession only of what passed since your last communicating, together with a general confession of your former sins, and a solemn renewing of your former acts of repentance, may serve the turn.

But if your conscience accuses you of any culpable neglect in your last examination, or of any great relapses, or of any wilful violations of your last vows and resolutions, in those, and the like cases, it is the surest way to begin all your repentance again.

Remember, Philotheus, that though it is God that works in you to will and to do of His good pleasure, yet God also commands you to work out your own salvation yourself, and therefore you are to labour for those blessings, and to practise those graces you pray for, so that you are to read your duty in your prayers.

If you find any particular sin you are guilty of, or any particular grace which you want, or any particular blessing which you are to give thanks for, which is not here mentioned, it is easier for you to add it to your prayers as occasion requires; in like manner, if you meet with any passage, in any prayer, which does not either so directly, or so fully express the sense of your soul, as you could wish, leave it out.

If opportunity, leisure, and devotion altogether, do at any time when you go home, or at times of liberty, incline you to make some present addition to your daily prayers, or like Daniel and holy David,[1] not only at morning and at evening, but at noon-day, to pray to God, thou mayest then use the prayer for particular graces,[m] or those acts of resolution and oblation,[n] or on Sunday and holydays the form of general thanksgiving, or on fasting days, the form of general intercession, as may best suit with the season, and with your own affections.

DIRECTIONS CONCERNING INFIRMITIES.

If after all the care and pains you can take,

[1] Dan. vi. 10.; Ps. lv. 17.   m Page 67.
n Page 64—66.

and your petitions also for God's grace, you find in the performance of any duty, in your daily prayers, examinations, receiving the Holy Eucharist, or the like, great coldness, and wanderings, and incomposedness, and weariness of spirit, and that your heart is little affected with it, and that you fall very much short of rules here laid down, and therefore ready to conclude, that all you have done is in vain, and displeasing to God :

Be not disheartened at this, Philotheus. It is a good sign to be so much grieved for your failings in your duty ; it is an argument of a filial tenderness, and desire to serve God better, that your spirit is willing though your flesh is weak ; and if you still continue your endeavours and prayers, patiently relying on God's infinite goodness, and on His gracious promise of hearing you, He will assuredly hear you in His good time.

Know, good Philotheus, that this is the case of thousands, as well as of yourself : the very best of Christians sigh under the perverseness and impotence of their corrupt nature, and

even the just man falls seven times a day,
through sins of ignorance, or infirmity, or
sudden surreption, or inadvertency, or the
like; though it is true, he riseth again by an
habitual repentance: and therefore be not
discouraged, but daily beg pardon for your
daily failings.

To ease you in such indispositions, or when
you are also straitened in time, or diverted by
any unavoidable avocations, I advise you to
shorten your prayers, and for the longer morning and evening prayer, say the shorter; and
as for the other parts of devotion throughout
this whole Manual, they are cut into so many
breaks and divisions, on purpose that you may
lengthen or shorten your prayers, as may best
comply with your occasions and infirmities;
only let me warn you seriously, that under
colour of indulging your infirmities, you do not
indulge your sloth.

Be not then afflicted, good Philotheus, if
you cannot come up exactly to the rules here
given you. Believe me, it was never imagined
you would; it was only hoped that you would

endeavour it : and know that it is a great error
of many devout souls to think all they do sig-
nifies nothing, because they fall short of the
rules laid down in their books of devotion;
little considering that it is sincerity God
requires of us, and not perfection, for if there
be a willing mind in us, it is accepted according
to that which a man hath, and not according
to that a man hath not;° so that your infirmities ought to humble, but not discourage
you.

For instance, suppose you should not be
able after all your endeavours and prayers, to
shed any or but few tears for your sins, be not
too much cast down at it; for to be troubled
for want of tears, is one sign of godly sorrow :
and it is certain, though tears are very desir-
able, yet they are not always signs of true
repentance, for hypocrites may shed them, and
there may be true godly sorrow without them ;
and perhaps God will at last give them to you,
when His wisdom sees your heart in a fit tem-
per for them.

o 2 Cor. viii. 12.

Whensoever then you are troubled with an afflicting sense of your infirmities, and for your many failings, I advise you to say this prayer following, and to rest satisfied that He that died for you, will both hear, and accept, and succour you.

A Prayer against Failings.

O Thou compassionate Saviour of sinful men, look down from heaven, and have mercy upon me, wretched sinner : O save me, O help me, for without Thee I can do nothing as I ought !

Miserable man that I am, my very prayers and repentance are accompanied with so many failings, that I am sometimes afraid that Thou, Lord, wilt not hear such prayers, nor regard such repentance !

But, O blessed Saviour, my Lord, and my God, it is Thy promise, not to discourage the least measure of grace. Thou wilt not quench the smoking flax, or break the bruised reed. q

It is Thy practice, Lord, to comply with the weakness of Thy servants. Thou art the

p Matt. xii. 20.

good Shepherd who carriest the tender lambs in Thy very bosom, and gently leadest those that be with young ! p

Nay, Lord, it is Thy very nature so to do, for Thou Thyself hast felt human infirmities, and canst not but commiserate those that sigh under them ! q

Why art thou then so heavy, O my soul, and why art thou so disquieted within me! O put thy trust in thy Saviour, who is the help of my countenance and my God r !

O gracious Lord, do Thou pity me and accept my weak and imperfect performances, and supply, by Thy boundless mercy, all the defects in my duty; and if it be Thy pleasure I should serve Thee better, O Lord God, increase Thy succours of grace, and I shall then increase my obedience !

O Thou lover of souls, for the sake of that infinite compassion of Thine, which moved Thee to die for me, hear me, and help me. Amen, Lord Jesus; Amen, Amen.

q Isa. xl. 11.   r Heb. ii. 18. iv. 15.
s Psalm xlii 5.

Directions in time of Sickness.

Far be it from you, good Philotheus, to counterfeit yourself sick at any time, to avoid the school, or the like, lest God send you sickness indeed to punish your idleness and dissimulation.

But if it please God to visit you with a real disease, let it be your first care to make your peace with Heaven; for God, by taking you off from your usual studies, does give you a call to repentance, and the examination of yourself in the beginning of your sickness is as seasonable and necessary as before your communicating; besides, if your sickness proves dangerous, you will then, I doubt not, desire to communicate, so that to fit you both for the Holy Sacrament, and for heaven, examination and repentance ought to be first in your thoughts.

Beware, Philotheus, of deferring this duty, because you are young, and think you may have time enough to repent hereafter; for you see, that persons younger than yourself die, and you are not sure to outlive this distemper ; and if you should put it off till your sickness grows more on you, it may perhaps take away your senses ; or if it does not, be sure it will' much more indispose you to prayer and recollection.

In the beginning then of your sickness begin your repentance, and say over this following prayer, and not only say, but practise it.

Prayer in the beginning of Sickness.

O heavenly Father, Who in Thy wisdom knowest what is best for me, glory be to Thee.

Lord, if it seem good in Thy sight, divert this distemper from me, which I now feel seizing on me, that I may employ my health to Thy glory, and praise Thy name !

But if Thou art pleased it should grow on me, I willingly submit to Thy afflicting hand, for Thou art wont to chastise those whom Thou dost love, and I am sure, Thou wilt lay no more on me, than Thou wilt enable me to bear[t].

I know, O my God, Thou sendest this

t 1 Cor. x. 13.

sickness on me for my good, even to humble and reform me; O grant it may work that saving effect in me.

Lord, create in me a true penitent sorrow for all my sins past, a steadfast faith in Thee, and sincere resolutions of amendment for the time to come.

Deliver me from all frowardness and impatience, and give me an entire resignation to Thy divine will : O suffer not the disease to take away my senses, and do Thou continually supply my thoughts with holy ejaculations ; Lord, bless all means that are used for my recovery, and restore me to my health in Thy good time ; but if otherwise Thou hast appointed for me, Thy blessed will be done. O wean my affections from all things below, and fill me with ardent desires after heaven: Lord, fit me for Thyself, and then call me to those joys unspeakable and full of glory, when Thou pleasest, and that for the sake of thy only Son Jesus, my Saviour, in whose holy words I sum up all my wants : Our Father, &c.

Ejaculations in time of Sickness.

Father, if it be possible remove this cup from me; nevertheless not my will but thine be done[t].

Trouble and heaviness have taken hold on me, but my sure trust is in Thee, O Lord!

Forsake me not, O my God, when my strength faileth me; haste Thee to help me, O Lord God of my salvation[u]!

Lord, teach me so to number my days that I may apply my heart to wisdom[x].

Deal thou with me, O Lord, according to Thy name, for sweet is Thy mercy.

Lord, what is my hope! truly my hope is even in Thee.

O my soul, tarry thou the Lord's leisure, be strong and He shall comfort thy heart, and put thou thy trust in the Lord[y]!

Into thy hands I commend my spirit, for Thou hast redeemed me, O Lord, thou God of truth.

t Matt. xxvi. 39.   u Psalm xxxvii. 21. 22.
x Psalm xc. 12.   y Psalm xxvii. 16.

In my Father's house are many mansions, and Thou, Lord Jesus, art gone before to prepare the place for us, that where Thou art we may be also[z]!

Lord, be merciful to me a miserable sinner.

O Lord God, we must all at the last day appear before Thy judgment-seat; O cleanse me from my sins, that I may be found blameless at the coming of the Lord Jesus!

As the day goeth away, and the shadows of the evening are stretched out, so passeth away my life, even like a vapour, that appeareth for a little time, and vanisheth away[a]!

Eye hath not seen, nor ear heard, nor the heart of man conceived, the good things which God hath laid up for those that love Him. Lord, do thou therefore inflame my soul with Thy love[b]!

I know, Lord, that thy judgments are right, and Thou of very faithfulness hast caused me to be troubled[c].

z John xiv. 2. a Jer. vii. ; James iv. 14.
b 1 Cor. ii. 9. c Psalm cxix. 75

O heavenly Father, my hope is wholly in Thy mercy, and in the merits and sufferings of my Saviour, O for His sake forgive and save me!

To these and the like ejaculations, Philotheus, which thou mayest gather thyself, thou mayest now and then either read a Psalm yourself, or have one read to you, as particularly the 23rd or 25th, or 27th or 51st, or any other that does best suit with thy condition.

I need give you no farther directions for the time of sickness, because I presume, Philotheus, that when you feel your sickness prevailing on you, you will then send for a spiritual guide, who will give you more particular advice, and minister to all the necessities of your soul, and therefore I shall only add this form of thanksgiving.

A THANKSGIVING FOR RECOVERY.

Glory be to Thee, O heavenly Father, for the sickness Thou hast in mercy sent me!

Lord, the stripes Thou didst lay on me, were the stripes of love, glory be to Thee!

Before I was troubled, I went wrong, but now will I keep thy word[d].

It is good for me that I have been in trouble, that I might learn Thy statutes.

Glory be to Thee, O Lord, glory be to Thee, for delivering me from the terrors of death, aad restoring me to my health again, glory be to Thee!

I called upon the Lord in my trouble, and the Lord heard me at large[e]!

I shall not die but live, and declare the works of the Lord!

Praise the Lord therefore, O my soul, as long as I have my life, which at first God gave me, and which he has now restored to me, I will sing praise unto my God!

O Lord God, who hast in Thy tender mercy prolonged my days in this world, give me grace to spend that life Thou hast now lengthened in Thy service. O give me

d Psalm cxix. 67.　　　e Psalm cxviii. 5.

grace to perform all my resolutions of new obedience, and so to live in the filial fear of Thee all the remainder of my time, that I may at last die at peace with myself, at peace with the whole world, and at peace with Thee; and that for the sake of Thy well-beloved Son, and my Saviour, in whose holy words I sum up all my wants: Our Father, &c.

To this you may add, if you think fit, the hundred and third Psalm.

To conclude, good Philotheus, if you have reaped any good from these prayers and instructions, be sure to give God hearty thanks for it, and let this encourage you to make the more frequent use of them, and God of his infinite mercy bless them every day more and more to your growth in grace, and to His own glory. Amen.

THREE HYMNS

BY

THE AUTHOR OF THE MANUAL OF PRAYERS.

For the use of the Scholars of Winchester College. a

A MORNING HYMN.

Awake, my soul, and with the sun,
Thy daily stage of duty run;
Shake off dull sloth, and joyful rise,
To pay thy morning sacrifice.

a *Advertisement*—"Whereas at the end of a book lately
published, called, 'A Conference between the Soul and Body,
there are some Hymns said to be written by Bishop Ken"
who absolutely disowns them, as being very false and
uncorrect; but the genuine ones are to be had only of
Charles Brome, bookseller, whose just property the original
copy is."

Thy precious time mispent, redeem,
Each present day thy last esteem ;
Improve thy talent with due care,
For the great day thyself prepare.

In conversation be sincere,
Keep conscience as the noon-tide clear.
Think how all-seeing God thy ways,
And all thy secret thoughts surveys.

By influence of the light divine,
Let thy own light to others shine,
Reflect all heaven's propitious rays,
In ardent love, and cheerful praise.

'Wake, and lift up thyself my heart,
And with the angels bear thy part,
Who all night long unwearied sing,
High praise to the eternal King.

I wake, I wake, ye heavenly choir,
May your devotion me inspire,
That I like you my age may spend,
Like you may on my God attend.

May I like you on God delight,
Have all day long my God in sight,
Perform like you my Maker's will,
O may I never more do ill.

Had I your wings to heaven I'd fly,
But God shall that defect supply;
And my soul wing'd with warm desire,
Shall all day long to heaven aspire.

All praise to Thee, who safe hast kept,
And hast refresh'd me whilst I slept;
Grant, Lord, when I from death shall wake,
I may of endless light partake.

I would not wake, nor rise again,
Even heaven itself I would disdain,
Wert not Thou there to be enjoy'd,
And I in hymns to be employed.

Heav'n is, dear Lord, where e'er Thou art,
O never then from me depart:
For to my soul, 'tis hell to be,
But for one moment void of Thee.

Lord, I my vows to Thee renew;
Disperse my sins as morning dew:
Guard my first springs of thought and will,
And with Thyself my spirit fill.

Direct, control, suggest this day,
All I design, or do, or say;
That all my powers with all their might,
In Thy sole glory may unite.

Praise God from whom all blessings flow,
Praise Him all creatures here below,
Praise Him above ye heavenly host,
Praise Father, Son, and Holy Ghost.

AN EVENING HYMN.

ALL praise to Thee, my God, this night,
For all the blessings of the light,
Keep me, O keep me, King of kings,
Beneath thy own Almighty wings.

Forgive me, Lord, for Thy dear Son,
The ill that I this day have done;
That with the world, myself, and Thee,
I ere I sleep at peace may be.

Teach me to live, that I may dread
The grave as little as my bed;
To die, that this vile body may
Rise glorious at the awful day.

O may my soul on Thee repose,
And may sweet sleep mine eyelids close;
Sleep that may me more vig'rous make,
To serve my God when I awake.

When in the night I sleepless lie,
My soul with heavenly thoughts supply;
Let no ill dreams disturb my rest,
No power of darkness me molest.

Dull sleep of sense me to deprive,
I am but half my time alive;
Thy faithful lovers, Lord, are griev'd,
To lie so long of Thee bereav'd.

But tho' sleep o'er my frailty reigns,
Let it not hold me long in chains;
And now and then let loose my heart,
Till it an hallelujah dart.

The faster sleep the senses binds,
The more unfetter'd are our minds;
O may my soul from matter free,
Thy loveliness unclouded see!

O when shall I in endless day,
For ever chase dark sleep away,
And hymns with the supernal choir,
Incessant sing and never tire!

O may my Guardian while I sleep,
Close to my bed His vigils keep,
His love angelical instil,
Stop all the avenues of ill.

May He celestial joy rehearse,
And thought to thought with me converse,
Or in my stead, all the night long,
Sing to my God a grateful song.

Praise God from whom all blessings flow,
Praise Him all creatures here below,
Praise Him above ye heavenly host,
Praise Father, Son, and Holy Ghost.

A MIDNIGHT HYMN.

My God, now I from sleep awake,
The sole possession of me take;
From midnight terrors me secure,
And guard my heart from thoughts impure.

Bless'd angels! while we silent lie,
You hallelujahs sing on high;
You joyful hymn the ever bless'd,
Before the throne, and never rest.

I with your choir celestial join,
In offering up a hymn divine,
With you in heaven I hope to dwell,
And bid the night and world farewell.

My soul when I shake off this dust,
Lord, in Thy arms I will entrust;
O make me Thy peculiar care,
Some mansion for my soul prepare.

Give me a place at Thy saints' feet,
Or Some fall'n angel's vacant seat;
I'll strive to sing as loud as they,
Who sit above in brighter day.

O may I always ready stand,
With my lamp burning in my hand;
May I in sight of heav'n rejoice,
Whene'er I hear the bridegroom's voice.

All praise to Thee in light array'd,
Who light Thy dwellingplace hast made:
A boundless ocean of bright beams,
From Thy all-glorious Godhead streams.

The sun in its meridian height
Is very darkness in Thy sight!
My soul, O lighten and inflame,
With thought and love of Thy great name.

Blessed Jesu, Thou on heaven intent,
Whole nights hast in devotion spent;
But I, frail creature, soon am tir'd,
And all my zeal is soon expir'd.

My soul, how canst thou weary grow,
Of antedating bliss below;
In sacred hymns, and heavenly love,
Which will eternal be above.

Shine on me, Lord, new life impart,
Fresh ardours kindle in my heart;
One ray of Thy all quick'ning light,
Dispels the sloth and clouds of night.

Lord, lest the tempter me surprise,
Watch over thine own sacrifice;
All loose, all idle thoughts cast out,
And make my very dreams devout.

Praise God, from Whom all blessings flow,
Praise Him all creatures here below;
Praise Him above ye heavenly host,
Praise Father, Son, and Holy Ghost.